NORTH
AFRICAN
TEXTILES

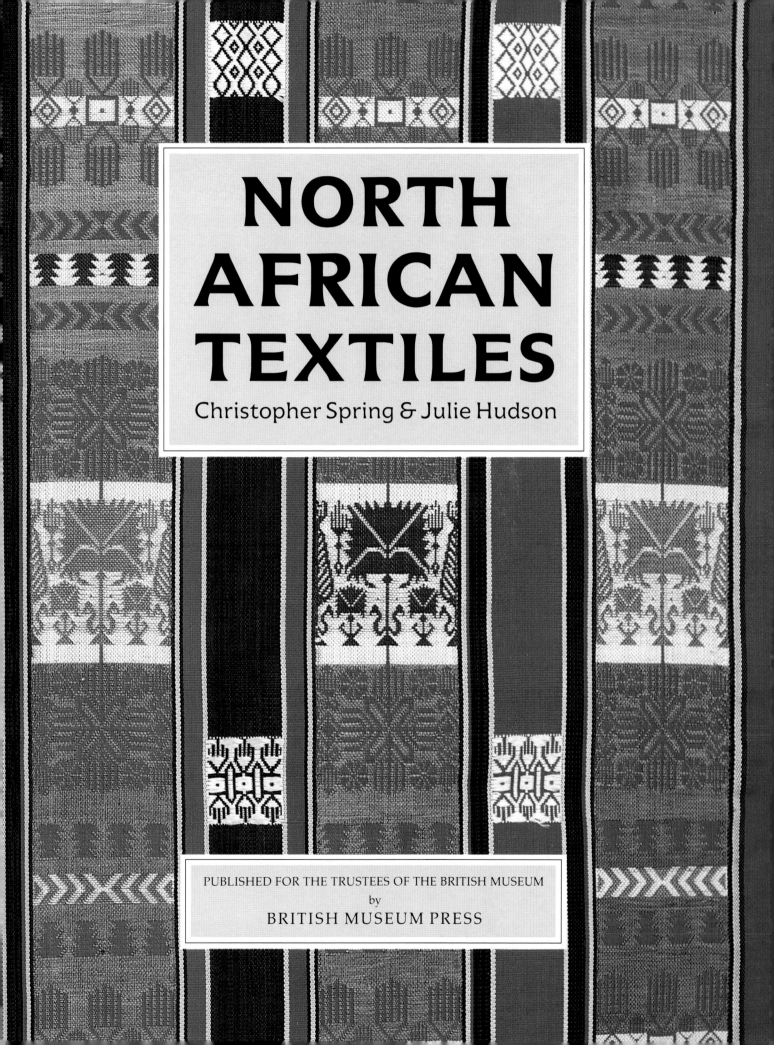

NORTH AFRICAN TEXTILES

Christopher Spring & Julie Hudson

PUBLISHED FOR THE TRUSTEES OF THE BRITISH MUSEUM
by
BRITISH MUSEUM PRESS

IN MEMORY OF RICHARD KEEN

Published by British Museum Press
A division of The British Museum Company Ltd
46 Bloomsbury Street
London WC1B 3QQ

Christopher Spring and Julie Hudson have asserted their right
to be identified as authors of this work

ISBN 0-7141-2523-7

A catalogue record for this book
is available from the British Library

Designed by Harry Green
Map by Hans Rashbrook
Photoset in Linotron Palatino by
Rowland Phototypesetting Ltd
Bury St Edmunds, Suffolk

Printed in Italy by Artegrafica, Verona

Cover Detail from the hem of a *mwashma*
(tattooed) tunic worn on the third day of marriage
in Raf-Raf, Tunisia (see p. 75).

Pages 2–3 Detail from a silk wedding veil.
Such cloths were used subsequently as wall-hangings
and shrouds in urban Tunisia.
L: 227 cm; W: 56 cm. 1907, 10–16.9.

CONTENTS

Acknowledgements
page 7

Preface
page 9

1
The Threads of
North African History
page 11

2
Food of the Loom
Raw Materials and Technology
page 27

3
The Patterns of Life
page 43

4
Display and Modesty
Textiles for Marriage
page 61

5
Textiles of Town and Country
page 83

6
Beyond the Loom
Non-woven Designs and Techniques
page 99

7
Secular and Sacred
The Textiles of Ethiopia
page 119

8
Continuity and Change
page 133

Bibliography
page 140

Glossary
page 142

Index
page 143

ACKNOWLEDGEMENTS

Numerous individuals and institutions helped directly or indirectly with the writing of this book and the research upon which it is based. We are grateful to them all, but we owe a particular debt of gratitude to the following: Shelagh Weir, Birgit Dohrendorf, Saul Peckham, Stephen Bell, Mike Row, Dave Agar, Dudley Hubbard, Yvonne Ayo, Jim Hamill, Yohannes Zeleke, Michael Spring, Sheila Paine, Wedad Hamed, James Bynon, John Harding, Roger Balsom, John Mellors, Mireille Morin-Barde, Jacke Phillips, Aidan Dodson and Salah el-Ghobashy.

Finally, we thank John Mack, without whose support and encouragement it would not have been possible to complete this book.

TRANSLITERATION NOTE
Arabic terms appear in the main text with no distinction made between light and emphatic consonants and long and short vowels. The consonant *'ain* is, however, indicated in the main text by ' and the glottal stop (*hamza*) by '. Diacritical signs are employed in the glossary. Standard Arabic terms are used wherever possible, although in some cases local dialect forms are retained. In these instances it has proved difficult to verify the correct transcription. The terms used are associated specifically with North African culture. However, their meanings may vary in other regions and in different contexts. Place names are employed according to widespread usage.

Detail from a wall or floor covering popularly known as *kilim trabelsi* recalling the origin of its weavers. Libyans from Tripolitania immigrated to the mining towns around Redeyef, in south-west Tunisia, shortly after the Italian occupation in 1912. The textiles produced by the women on vertical looms have distinctive geometric motifs based on triangles, chevrons and stepped patterns in predominantly orange, red, black, white and green. These are sometimes combined with zoomorphic elements such as the gazelles seen here. L:235 cm; w:120 cm. 1977,Af8.1.

7

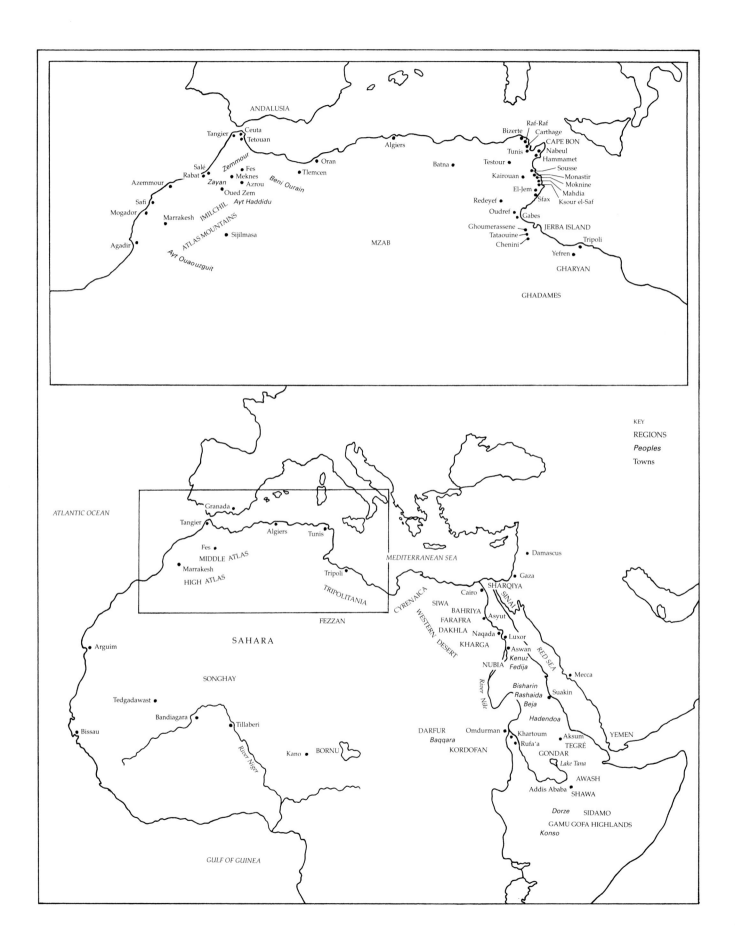

ANDALUSIA

Raf-Raf
Bizerte
Carthage
CAPE BON
Tangier · Ceuta
Tetouan
Tunis
Nabeul
Hammamet
Algiers
Testour
Sousse
Oran
Batna
Kairouan
Monastir
Salé
Zemmour
Fes
Moknine
Rabat
Zayan
Meknes
Azrou
El-Jem
Mahdia
Beni Ourain
Azemmour
Oued Zem
Redeyef
Sfax
Ksour el-Saf
Ayt Haddidu
Safi
Oudref
Gabes
Mogador
IMILCHIL
Marrakesh
Ghoumerassene
JERBA ISLAND
ATLAS MOUNTAINS
Tatouine
Tripoli
Tlemcen
Sijilmasa
Chenini
Agadir
Yefren
Ayt Ouaouzguit
MZAB
GHARYAN

GHADAMES

KEY

REGIONS

Peoples

Towns

ATLANTIC OCEAN
Granada
Tangier
Algiers
Tunis
Fes
Damascus
MEDITERRANEAN SEA
MIDDLE ATLAS
Gaza
Marrakesh
Tripoli
SHARQIYA
HIGH ATLAS
TRIPOLITANIA
Cairo
SINAI
SIWA
FEZZAN
CYRENAICA
BAHRIYA
SAHARA
FARAFRA
Asyut
DAKHLA
Naqada
Luxor
KHARGA
Aswan
Arguim
Kenuz
RED SEA
NUBIA
Fedija
Mecca
SONGHAY
Bisharin
Rashaida
Tedgadawast
Suakin
Beja
Bandiagara
River Nile
Tillaberi
Bissau
Hadendoa
DARFUR
Omdurman
YEMEN
Baqqara
Khartoum
Aksum
Kano
BORNU
River Niger
Rufa'a
TEGRÉ
KORDOFAN
GONDAR
Lake Tana
AWASH
Addis Ababa
SHAWA
Dorze
SIDAMO
GAMU GOFA HIGHLANDS
Konso
GULF OF GUINEA

PREFACE

It is now well over fifteen years since John Picton and I worked on a book entitled *African Textiles*, which is still in print. That book sought to deal – as the title implied – with Africa as a whole, and we were well aware that its virtues and failings were those of an introductory volume: it could not give equal weight and attention to all the weaving traditions of the continent. Likewise, in being largely based on the collections of a single institution (even one with substantial holdings) it was obliged to some extent to concentrate on those areas which were most strongly represented. However, we were always aware that more could be said, especially on the complex traditions of North and Northeast Africa.

Happily, this is now a situation which can be rectified. Over the past decade we have been fortunate to be able to develop both our curatorial expertise in this field and our holdings of textiles from the region. The result is this book, based on the research and fieldwork of two of our own staff, and on a wider selection of cloth than has previously been available to us for study and display. In common with our earlier survey, this book uses the term 'textile' in its broadest sense by including numerous techniques, materials and designs not directly associated with weaving, and by examining the significance of costume. However, whereas John Picton and I concentrated on the technological features of African weaving and textile decoration, this book looks to expand the subject in at least two desirable directions. One is towards giving due weight to the contemporary and urban contexts of textiles to the north of the Sahara; a second and related approach is in terms of the diverse symbolic and social world which textiles occupy.

The tendency has often been to interpret 'traditional' cloth and its production as a static phenomenon, resistant to change, and ultimately doomed to disappear before the advent of external modern influence. In Islamic, Christian and Jewish North Africa this is far from the case. Outside influence is by no means adopted wholesale, but likewise 'tradition' itself is not some piece of arcane intellectual and material baggage incapable of adapting. There is, in any case, no single formula applicable throughout a region of such cultural and religious diversity. This book seeks to explore some of these complexities, and thereby to add a new dimension to a subject which has long been a preoccupation of this Department of the British Museum.

JOHN MACK
Keeper of Ethnography

1

THE THREADS OF NORTH AFRICAN HISTORY

Woman's silk caftan with gold thread decoration from Fes, Morocco, collected in the mid-nineteenth century. Originating in Persia, caftans became popular throughout the Arab world. In North Africa they were worn by the urban elite and produced in vividly-coloured silks and brocades. L:132 cm; W:153 cm. 1984,Af6.1.

The Arabs called the region to the west of Egypt the *'maghrib'*, 'the place of sunset'; in contrast the Levant was known as 'the place of sunrise' (*mashriq*). The original Arab definition for the Maghrib was as the area bounded on the east by the Egyptian border, and enclosed by water on two sides: the Atlantic Ocean on the west and the Mediterranean Sea on the north, with the Sahara forming a less well-defined southern border. Writers and travellers have employed the term according to prevailing political interests in the area, thus reflecting the region's complex history and the diverse ethnicity of its populations; we will, however, employ the term in its original sense.

There existed a fragile pattern of coexistence between the intrusive foreign inhabitants, the founders of the urban centres, and the indigenous rural, 'tribal', communities. The complementary relationship established between the two elements was based partly on the rural population's ability to supply essential raw materials, balanced by the provision of processed goods by the towns.

This relationship was modified by the Arab invasion of the seventh century AD, since the conversion to Islam created not only a new sense of association between indigenes and invaders, but also a common focus for the different tribal groups. Willingness to accept Islam was further enhanced by the promise of economic reward for participation in Arab expansionist military activity.

Egypt and Sudan, bound together economically through their mutual reliance on the River Nile, are also linked in a cultural sense to the Maghrib. The geographical position of Egypt, linking the continents of Africa and Asia, has aided its establishment as an important centre for the introduction, assimilation and exchange of external elements. Following the spread of Islam in West Africa, it became a traditional stopping-off point for Muslims from northern Nigeria and beyond, on their annual pilgrimage to Mecca. The country retains a unique position belonging culturally neither to the Middle East nor to the Maghrib, although it manifests elements of both.

Detail from the hem of a dress worn by a woman of the Rashaida people, a nomadic group who emigrated from the Hijaz area of Saudi Arabia at the beginning of the nineteenth century, and today live around Suakin in the eastern Sudan. Their skirts are enlivened with bold appliqué patterns recalling the dress of Bedouin groups in Saudi Arabia. L:135 cm; W:240 cm. 1978,Af19.1.

North African History in Brief

North Africa occupies a key position in the Mediterranean basin; from ancient times it has served as a crossroads for peoples and influences moving northwards from sub-Saharan Africa, westwards from the Levant and southwards from Europe. The main indigenes, the Berbers, represent an amalgamation of the eastern Libu and the prehistoric inhabitants of the region. Although linked by their use of Berber dialects, they are neither politically nor racially homogeneous. They have inhabited a number of defined areas within a huge expanse of territory, from the Atlantic coast to Siwa Oasis, on the western border of Egypt.

With the exception of Egypt, where cultures may be traced back in detail to 5000 BC and beyond, the early history of North Africa is relatively obscure. Infiltration and threats of foreign entry into Egypt are attested in the third millennium BC, and specific conflicts are recorded in Egyptian sources in the thirteenth century BC. However, with the arrival of the Phoenicians in the eleventh century rather more becomes known. They established a string of trading posts along the North African coast marking out a route to Spain. Carthage was founded at the end of the ninth century BC by emigrants from Tyre, and in the fifth century emerged as the wealthy and flourishing capital of a new empire, with the Phoenician trading posts and other inland settlements under its leadership. Following their defeat in Sicily at the hands of the Greeks, the Carthaginians concentrated upon expanding their economic interests in North Africa.

Whilst under their control, trans-Saharan trade routes were exploited which originated in Egypt, Cyrenaica and Tripolitania and ran into the African hinterland; precious stones (carbuncles) were the principal recorded imports into North Africa at this period. There is also evidence of sea-borne expeditions down the Atlantic coast, possibly reaching as far as the Ivory Coast, where pottery was traded in exchange for animal hides and gold. However, this merchant empire suffered eventual destruction at the hands of the Romans in 146 BC, when Carthage was captured and its territories ultimately annexed to the new international power. The period of Roman rule heralded an upsurge in trans-Saharan trading activity, the regular use of camel transport helping to stimulate the development of new routes, especially those connected with the valuable gold trade. The continued trade in carbuncles was possibly combined with that of slaves by the third century AD, in exchange for pottery, glass, cloth, wine and olive oil, which were received by the Garamantes (an independent community settled in the oases of the Libyan Fezzan). By the fourth century, ivory was being traded into North Africa across the Sahara.

Even during this period of their unprecedented dominion, the Roman rulers encountered pockets of resistance from the Berber population, mainly in the inaccessible mountainous districts where local chiefs retained control. These groups coalesced to form raiding parties which succeeded in causing considerable internal disruption. Carthage, the long-established centre of political control, under first the Phoenicians and then the Romans, was reduced to the role of merely a strategically important port after its capture by the Germanic Vandals in AD 439, and their subsequent overthrow by the Byzantines under the Emperor Justinian in AD 533. North Africa thus became part of the Eastern Roman Empire, centred on Constantinople (Byzantium).

Christianity had been widespread in North Africa since the third century AD; however, in AD 639, Arab armies emerged from the eastern deserts, to overthrow Byzantine rule throughout North Africa and the Levant. The Arabs were initially aided in Egypt by the Coptic Christian community; this conquest marked the start of the gradual spread of Islam in North Africa, and thus heralded a new historic era.

The conversion to Islam, and the westward establishment of Arab control, was at first hindered by the resistance of the indigenous Berber-speaking populations; only when sufficiently large numbers of these groups had capitulated could the Arab armies establish control in North Africa. Berbers who had converted to Islam then formed the nucleus of the armies which, after advancing through North Africa, crossed from Tangier to Spain where they continued their conquest.

One of the most important factors in restoring commercial prosperity to North Africa following this upheaval was the trading activity of the Kharijites (a religious and politically-motivated group who believed that authority came only from God). Based in southern Tunisia and Tripolitania, during the ninth century they penetrated south as far as Awdaghast (modern Tedgadawast), a major centre on the western Saharan trading route, where they acquired gold while also supplying Egypt and Ifriqiya with slaves from the Central Sudan. Extensive trade networks thus ran from Spain through the Maghrib to Egypt, onwards to Syria, and also to India via the Red Sea; these were in addition to the numerous trans-Saharan routes.

The tenth century was marked by conflict between the Fatimids, based in Mahdia (Tunisia), and the Umayyad dynasty in Spain, leading to unrest and division in the area of northern Morocco and western Algeria. The Fatimid conquest of Egypt in AD 969 led to the establishment of a new regional capital by the Caliph al-Mu'izz: *al-Qahira al-Mu'izziya* (Cairo). Their puppet rulers in the Maghrib, the Zirids, however, had difficulties in maintaining control and, after breaking their allegiance to the Fatimids, their political instability was an

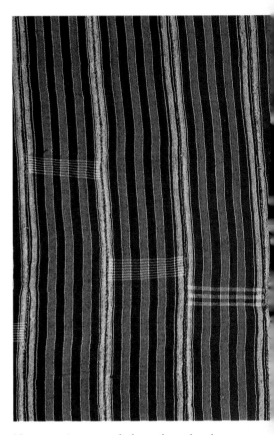

Narrow-strip cotton cloth used as a head covering in Ghadames Oasis, Libya. It is reminiscent of cloths from northern Nigeria and possibly originated there. Ghadames used to be an important centre on the trans-Saharan trade routes. Today there is a resident Hausa-speaking (northern Nigerian) community.
L:400 cm; w:130 cm. 1981,Af5.11.

LEFT Shawl (*derfudit*) worn by women of Siwa Oasis, Egypt, on leaving their homes. For generations, the blue and white checked base material has been imported from the village of Kerdassa, near Cairo. Until the 1920s the caravan route linking Cairo with Siwa began at Kerdassa. L:100 cm; w:155 cm. 1991,Af11.3.

The women of the Mesguita, Morocco, are unusual in wearing brightly coloured gathered skirts over the top of their draped garments. The name of the skirt, *faltita*, points to a possible Hispanic origin: in Spanish *falda* is the word for a skirt. *Photo: M. Morin-Barde.*

invitation to infiltration by foreign elements. Thus, the Arab Banu Hilal and Banu Sulaim tribes, encouraged by the Egyptian Fatimid dynasty, seized the opportunity to invade the Maghrib from the east in 1052, while the Sanhaja Berbers (Almoravids) invaded from the western Sahara. The latter group succeeded in founding Marrakesh in 1060 under the leadership of Abu Bakr, whose cousin and successor Yusuf ibn Tashfin conquered north-west Africa and Muslim Spain, following the collapse of the Umayyad dynasty.

As in earlier times, the rebellious Berber tribes of the High Atlas (Morocco) challenged this new authority; the Almohads, the 'Unitarians' (*al-muwahhidun*), were led by Ibn Tumart, who was popularly regarded as the new Mahdi (the rightly guided one). By 1147 Marrakesh had fallen and an Almohad dynasty was established there under Ibn Tumart's successor 'Abd al-Mu'min, who extended its rule into North Africa as far as Tripoli, and later into Muslim Spain. The dynasty enjoyed immense prosperity and the arts and sciences flourished, despite the asceticism of the movement's leaders.

By the beginning of the thirteenth century the Almohad empire was weakening, culminating in a defeat by the Christians of Castile (Spain) in 1212. The death of the Almohad Caliph al-Nasir in 1213 led to a series of internal battles between the ruling dynasty and the Banu Marin, a Berber group, who became the founders of the Marinid state. The Hafsids, claiming legitimacy as the rightful heirs of the Almohads, continued to exert a limited sphere of power within Ifriqiya, but Muslim Spain, with the exception of Granada, reverted to the control of Portugal, Castile and Aragon. A steady flow of Andalusian Muslims emigrated to Morocco from this period until the fall of Granada in 1492.

Portuguese settlements were established down the Atlantic coast of Morocco between 1458 and 1514, to take advantage of seaward access to the southern gold trade, while the Spanish occupied a string of Mediterranean coastal bases. However, this activity was eventually halted by the North African corsairs, working on behalf of the Ottomans, who had begun to establish themselves as a significant power in Algeria in 1516. It was not until 1525, however, that

Algiers finally came under Ottoman authority, and it was from this base that they extended their power, conquering Tripoli and then Tunis in 1574. Egypt had already been invaded and annexed in 1517. The modern divisions of Algeria, Tunisia and Libya were essentially established in 1587 when the regencies of Algiers, Tunis and Tripoli were created under the authority of the Ottoman Empire. Morocco alone resisted Turkish advances under the Sa'dians, led by the monarch Ahmad al-Mansur (1578–1603), who created an immensely wealthy and powerful kingdom. A successful expedition conquered Songhay in 1591; however, on Ahmad's death Morocco was once more divided and thus weakened politically.

During the seventeenth century the Ottoman regencies attempted to gain their independence; the power of administrative officials, the Pashas, appointed by the Ottoman Sultan, was diminished and wars between Morocco and the regencies at the end of the century resulted in the emergence of a series of essentially independent states.

The economic importance of the Maghrib had been undermined from the sixteenth century onwards by the discovery of sea routes to the Americas and the Indies. However, by the eighteenth century this was partly compensated for by a growing demand for North African grain exports and the revival of interest in the trans-Saharan trade routes, concentrated on the burgeoning states of Bornu and Waday. European merchants residing in the Maghrib and Egypt during this period amassed greater political power in line with the increasingly dominant role their native countries were displaying in the region. The turning-point in the relationship between Europe and the Maghrib came through the capture of Algiers in 1830 and the subsequent establishment of permanent settlements by French colonists in the following years. Tunisia became a French protectorate in 1881. Morocco proved more resistant to European advances; it was not until 1912 that Sultan Mulai Hafid accepted French protection for the bulk of the country, while the Spanish established a smaller protectorate along the Mediterranean coast.

Egypt had thrown off any effective central Ottoman control in the early nineteenth century, under the Pasha, Muhammad Ali. However, following the bankruptcy of his successsor, the Viceroy Ismail, Anglo-French control over the country's finances severely damaged its independence. European (essentially British) control was assured by the landing of troops in 1882 in reaction to a nationalist coup, predicated on the overwhelming strategic interest of the Suez Canal. Although only a formal protectorate from 1914 to 1922, British influence was paramount in Egypt until after the Second World War.

The North African countries, through the participation of their respective colonial or occupying powers, were active in the Second World War. Following this involvement, and possibly inspired by it, came increasing demands for political change. Anti-European uprisings, in addition to pressure from Russia and America, as well as from amongst the powers' own populations, eventually led to the instigation of agreements for the devolution of political power to the North African states, and ultimately real independence.

Precious Wool and Splendid Robes

Textiles have long played an important role in the economic and political life of North African countries. They have been used as declarations of status, bestowed as honorary gifts and displayed prominently at significant life-cycle

Mid-nineteenth-century cloth from Fes, Morocco, characterised by formally arranged geometric and stylised floral elements in monochrome purple silk. These cloths were produced for use on furnishings such as cushions, curtains, towels and mattress covers and were frequently embroidered in the home. L:104 cm; w:79 cm. 1916,8-5.1.

ceremonies. Changes in political power and the influence of foreign styles and fashions can be discerned in the cut and decoration of garments, especially among the urban elite. The extensive internal trade networks enabled clothing items and costly materials to obtain widespread impact.

The use of robes with figurative and geometric decoration was known in ancient Egypt, where they were associated with the court and specifically the ruler. A considerable quantity of clothing was discovered in the tomb of Tutankhamun, including the famous tunic in the Egyptian Museum (Cairo JE 62626), which Howard Carter described as 'a linen dalmatic decorated with tapestry-woven and needlework ornament' (1933: caption pl.39). Subsequent examination revealed that the woven strips were in a warp-faced weave, while the front and back borders and the cross-form on the chest were composed of embroidered bands. These appear to have been worked separately and then sewn to the linen tunic. Except for the collar, which displays cartouches bearing the prenomen of the king, the woven panels carry simple geometric patterns. The designs on the embroidered bands, however, depict winged female sphinxes, griffins and elaborate palmettes which seem to suggest Syrian influence, juxtaposed with Egyptian-inspired hunting scenes, themselves imbued with a Mesopotamian-style aggression. The ability to syncretise foreign elements while retaining a locally-recognised identity continues to be one of the most important factors sustaining North African culture.

Many extant early textiles, dating from the third or fourth century AD, come from Egypt and are popularly designated as Coptic. The term encompasses garments and cloths bearing patterns showing Greek and Byzantine influence, together with those produced after the Arab conquest. Coptic linen or woollen tunics are of a basic T-shape, some being decorated with tapestry-woven

RIGHT Detail of the embroidered panels forming the front border on the tunic of Tutankhamun (Cairo JE 62626). The patterns are enclosed within squares, each of which was sewn to the next before being applied to the tunic. The designs draw on Syrian motifs such as the palmette and the griffin, and hunting scenes which suggest Mesopotamian inspiration in their treatment. *Photo: Courtesy of The Egypt Exploration Society.*

ABOVE Part of a child's plain woollen tunic from Egypt, sixth to eighth century AD. Tapestry-woven stripes in purple wool and undyed flax decorate the shoulder and sleeve bands. *Photo: Courtesy of the Visitors of the Ashmolean Museum, Oxford.*

vertical stripes (a feature developed from the *clavi*, which acted as markers of rank on Roman clothing) many of which have additional figural ornamentation. However, although certain stylistic features were retained after the arrival of the Arabs, the exuberant plant and animal motifs were gradually replaced by inscriptions and geometric patterns.

In early Islamic society, where the value of clothing and textiles was of consummate importance, gifts of costume items were used frequently as a means of reward, or as an indication of court esteem. The Prophet Muhammad bestowed upon his favourites prestigious robes of honour. At this time the use of silk and gold by men was proscribed: the Qur'an, however, promised those who led blameless lives the luxury of silk garments in Paradise. These prohibitions were relaxed as the Islamic empire prospered and a wealthy elite class emerged, with a taste for opulence and splendour.

Under the Umayyads and Abbasids, royal textile production was formalised as a palace institution. Gifts of robes of honour (*khila'*) and cloths were frequently bestowed upon members of the court in recognition of their ser-

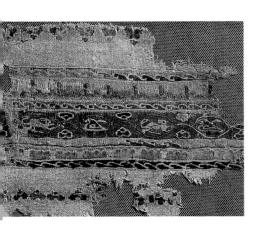

Fragment from the border of a linen cloth, found in Egypt during the Fatimid period, eleventh to twelfth centuries AD. The tapestry-woven decoration depicts figures of animals and birds in linen and silk thread.
Photo: The Whitworth Art Gallery, The University of Manchester.

vices, given to officials as a means of reward or presented during inauguration ceremonies; these cloths conferred status on the recipient. Workshops (*dar al-tiraz*) were established within the palace precincts in order to manufacture textiles reserved exclusively for the royal household. These opulent cloths were distinguished by bands of embroidered or woven inscription (*tiraz*), in gold or coloured thread. Frequently, the name of the current ruler, or a message in praise of God, was inscribed upon them.

During these periods of Muslim domination, textile factories flourished throughout the Arab empire and evidence of *tiraz* production may be found in Egypt, the Maghrib and Spain. Wealth, among the elite, was measured in terms of textile possessions, some of which would be handed down from parent to child. An inventory produced in 809 AD for the Caliph al-Amin eloquently highlights this preoccupation with the acquisition of textiles. It enumerated '8,000 *jubbahs* (coats), half of which were silk lined with sable, fox or goat hair, and the other half figured cloth (*washshi*); 10,000 shirts and tunics; 1,000 pairs of pants [trousers]; 10,000 caftans, 4,000 turbans; and 1,000 cloaks' (Golombek 1988:28). The significance and prominence of such fabrics continued under the hedonistic Fatimid dynasty, whose early rulers showered officials and their relatives with costly clothes and textiles. One of these courtiers, the controller of the *diwan al-majlis* (office of the council) acquired on the occasion of '*id al-fitr* (the feast of breaking the fast) 'a complete suit of gold-embroidered clothes, and a suit of silk clothes for his children. For the people of his household he received a gold-embroidered cloak . . . ' (Serjeant 1948:111). These 'gifts' of clothes were additional benefits attached to particular offices. However, the decline of the power of the Fatimids and the rise of the Almohads signalled a break with the institution of the *tiraz* factories. According to the historian Ibn Khaldun (1332–1406), the sumptuous garments and splendid textiles associated with previous regimes were abandoned by the Almohad rulers. The use of silk and gold by men was proscribed temporarily, in line with their adherence to purist ideals (Slane 1862–8:66). However, towards the end of this dynasty, luxury textiles were once more introduced, with a restricted use of figured decoration (Dodds 1992:109).

In addition to the textiles produced in their palace factories, Muslim rulers also exacted tribute in the form of garments and fine cloths. The Umayyad rulers possibly received 'the napkins (mandil) of Misr [Egypt] which are like the white skin inside eggshells' as part of this payment. These inhabitants were also obliged to provide their Arab conquerors with 'a woolen [sic] upper gown (djubba suf), an upper cloak (burnus) or turban ('imama), trousers (sarawil), and a pair of shoes a year' (Serjeant 1948:89).

The immense quantity of textiles produced during the period of Arab dominion was not reserved entirely for the rulers and their entourage: there is also abundant evidence for an active market in 'domestic' textiles throughout North Africa and Spain. Several cities and towns possessed public textile factories (*tiraz al-'amm*); the Arab geographer Idrisi, writing in the twelfth century, described the textile industry in Bahnasa (Egypt): 'in it [Bahnasa] are many *tiraz* factories belonging to the public ('*amma*), where the merchants evaluate the precious curtains . . . These curtains, carpets (*fursh*) and robes are renowned throughout the earth' (Serjeant 1948:108).

In Morocco, the city most famed for its textile production during the period of Muslim control was Fes. The town certainly possessed *tiraz* factories, although it has been suggested that these operated independently of the sovereign (Serjeant 1951:51). Even towards the end of the purist Almohad dynasty, the city supported '467 funduks (inns for merchants) . . . 3094 houses of tiraz (atriza) . . . and 116 dyehouses . . . inside the walls' (Serjeant 1951:51). The city prospered, especially in the fields of arts and crafts which had been stimulated by Andalusian influences since the Almoravid era. It appears that weaving constituted the most important industry in the capital under the Marinids, with about 20,000 persons occupied in this pursuit. Abun-Nasr notes that the annual pilgrimage to Mecca 'was the occasion for selling the goods of Fez in eastern countries . . . these goods also reached the Niger bend by way of the caravan route starting in Sijilmasa'(1975:136).

Other North African countries were recognised for the excellence of their textile industries; al-Tijani, an official writing between AD 1306–1309, extols the quality of the raw materials available on the island of Jerba (Tunisia): 'this island is famous in other countries for the superior quality of the wool that its numerous flocks produce. In no other part of Africa are finer kinds for the weaving of rich stuffs and garments to be found' (Rousseau 1852:171). However, the Syrian official al-'Umari (1301–1349), laments the choice of dress of the citizens of Ifriqiya who 'wear clothes of wool and cotton. Those who wear elegant clothing from Alexandria are isolated individuals' (Sergeant 1951:41). It is notable that this author resided for many years in Egypt, where his father was a senior member of the Mamluk chancellery: hence his views may be coloured by his own luxurious upbringing (Levtzion and Hopkins 1981:252).

Thus, by the time of the Ottoman expansion into North Africa during the sixteenth century, the region had already experienced a wide interchange of textile influences, styles and materials. Turkish modes of dress were easily integrated into the existing elite clothing repertoire. The most detailed and reliable sources for descriptions of these urban costumes were produced by Europeans during the nineteenth century. One of the finest accounts was written by Edward Lane, who lived in Cairo from 1825 until 1849. At this period the female upper classes throughout the Near East and North Africa displayed a certain level of consistency in dress, through their similar use of multitudinous layers of fine clothing. Lane (1871 vol. 1:53, 55) describes the costume of a wealthy woman:

Over the shirt and shintiyan [trousers] is worn a long vest (called 'yelek') . . . A square shawl, or an embroidered kerchief, doubled diagonally, is put loosely round the waist as a girdle . . . Over the yelek is worn a gibbeh [outer garment] of cloth, or velvet, or silk, usually embroidered with gold or with coloured silk . . . Whenever a lady leaves the house, she wears, in addition . . . a large, loose gown . . . it is of silk; generally of a pink, or rose, or violet colour. Next is put on the 'burko', or face-veil . . . The lady then covers herself with a 'habarah' [cloak], . . . of glossy, black silk.

The period from the late nineteenth century until the beginning of the twentieth century was dominated by an increase in European economic influence and control. Once again, the fluctuating political situation was reflected in the appearance of innovative dress styles, inspired by European – especially Parisian – fashions. Young girls from wealthy backgrounds were placed under the tutelage of Western governesses, who taught European languages and music to their pupils. Several of these teachers wrote fascinating accounts of their interaction with female members of elite families, and

The Princess Zaynab, daughter of Ismail Pasha of Egypt. Her European-style outfit dates to around the 1880s. Typical of clothing of this period is the high neckline and the buttoned ankle boots embellished with rosettes. Her pose and hairstyle recall those of young ladies of fashion in Europe at this period. From E. Chennells, *Recollections of an Egyptian Princess by her English governess*, London, 1893.

Wool and goat hair textile (*kerka*) from Tillaberi in Niger, used as a tent divider or hung over the marriage bed. It is woven in strips which are sewn together so that the pattern runs horizontally. The cross, lozenge and triangle patterns recall those used on North African cloths. L:329 cm; w:138 cm. 1978,Af21.1.

recorded the emergence and growing impact of European dress fashions. The Khedive Ismail's daughter Zaynab was taught by Ellen Chennells towards the end of the nineteenth century. She described the princess's costume: '[she] was magnificently dressed in black velvet, made in the last Parisian fashion. The trimming was of white ostrich feathers . . . She wore . . . black velvet boots with diamond buckles, and a velvet hat with the same feather trimming as on the dress' (1893:27).

The Impact of Trade

Even though the cultures of North Africa and sub-Saharan Africa are rarely discussed *in tandem*, there is some archaeological and ethnographic evidence for textile exchange, and the direct borrowing and imitation of designs between these two areas. Unfortunately, evidence for the history of trade across the trans-Saharan routes prior to the Arab invasion of North Africa is limited. Herodotus, writing in the fifth century BC, described the travels of Nasamonian princes who reached the bend of the Niger River from Libya: 'they travelled over the desert, towards the west, and crossed a wide sandy area . . . ' (Godley 1926:313). Carthaginian commercial enterprises in the fifth century BC began in the same area (Tripolitania), with trade routes running across the Sahara. The emergence of personal accounts of journeys throughout North and West Africa from Arab writers and travellers provides a clearer picture of the extent of the

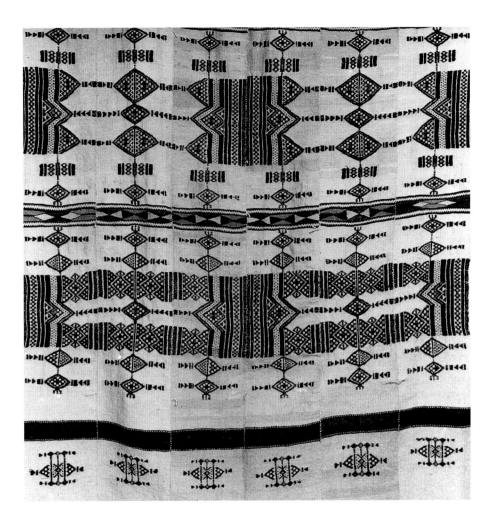

Unlike North African cloths which are woven on a wide loom, these wool and goat hair blankets (*kaasa*) from Mali are produced on the double-heddle, narrow-strip loom. However, the separate strips are subsequently sewn together ensuring that the weft designs line up to give an impression of continuous bands of pattern. The geometric motifs may have been influenced by North African patterns, made familiar to Malian weavers through trading links. L:237 cm; w:131 cm. 1980,Af38.1.

trading networks and the sort of goods available. In the eleventh century, the Arab writer al-Bakri comments briefly that wool goods were exported from the coast at Barka (modern Libya). Several centuries later, and further to the west, Ibn Khaldun recorded the movement of wool south from Sijilmasa (Morocco). Iwalatan is described by Ibn Battuta in the fourteenth century as: 'two complete months away from Sijilmasa and the first place in the negro country . . . The garments of its inhabitants are lovely and imported from Egypt' (Serjeant 1951:54). Thus, although incomplete and covering a huge span of time, documentary material seems to suggest the presence of early trans-Saharan trade routes, carrying both raw materials and cloths to the south.

Owing to their perishable nature, few early textile examples have emerged. However, cloth fragments were discovered in the burial caves at Bandiagara (Mali), dating from the eleventh century AD. In addition to narrow-strip cotton cloths, presumably locally produced, there were wider examples in wool, which may indicate a North African origin. The woollen examples also bear geometric patterns recalling those on rural textiles of the Maghrib, such as the cross, triangle and vertical bar. It is tempting to view this deposit, with its range of techniques and design features, as early evidence of a trade in cloth between North and sub-Saharan Africa.

The woollen cloths produced around the region of the Niger bend (Mali) bear striking patterns which recall design elements used by rural weavers in North

Africa for their flat-woven shawls and coverings. As with the Berber motifs, the pattern elements are named. These names may have varied meanings throughout the area, or may be applied to different combinations of geometric forms. The patterns recall physical elements in the local environment and are named accordingly; the most widely accepted forms include *bidal* 'family compound', *togguere*, 'hillocks', *tiouke*, 'unripe fruit' and *bitjirgal* 'water recipient'. The last pattern is often the first design to be woven onto a blanket; the weavers view it as a symbol of fertility and maternity (Imperato 1973:45–6). The cloths produced have specific purposes; the *kaasa* is used as a protective cover, sheltering its owner from the harsh heat as well as the bitter cold. In addition, it acts as a mosquito net, the thickness of the cover preventing penetration. The *kerka* is an exquisitely-woven woollen cloth, produced on the occasion of a wedding. It is also used as protection against the ravages of mosquitos, being suspended over the bed at night. These cloths are composed of narrow strips sewn together, unlike the single widths of Berber textiles. However, it is possible that inspiration for the geometric designs may have come from North Africa, as a result of earlier imports.

The first Europeans to infiltrate the trading market established between West and North Africa were the Portuguese, who, between 1480 and 1540, controlled the Atlantic coastline from Morocco to the Guinea gulf. They engaged in a profitable trade with West Africa, exchanging copper and cloth in particular for slaves and gold, thus successfully eliminating the Sahara middlemen. They maintained a string of trading stations and distribution centres around western Morocco, which included Tangier, Ceuta, Mogador, Agadir and Safi, with an isolated post at Arguim on the Saharan coast. For centuries North African cloth had been traded south through the trans-Saharan routes; the Portuguese quickly realised the commercial potential in supplying an eager West African population with these prestigious woollen cloths via the seaward route. Their success in this area was secured by their ability to supply the three most popular types of cloth: *aljaravias*, *alquices* and *lambens*.

By the late sixteenth century the Portuguese, under King John II, claimed exclusive jurisdiction over the Guinea coast. The ease of access via the seaward routes boosted the demand for textiles at an unprecedented rate. The weavers from the village of Mazouna near Oran (Algeria), who supplied the most popular designs, were unable to meet the requirements of this textile boom. Thus, these cloths retained their prestige value throughout the period of Portuguese domination, due to their scarcity. The trading posts at Oran and Safi feature prominently in written records of this time as places where huge quantities of *lambens* were purchased and exported. Such was the demand for North African cloths, that in 1507 a permanent weaving house was established in Safi, designed primarily to manufacture *lambens* of suitable quality for export to West Africa. The hooded cloak (*aljaravias*) had also found popularity in West Africa. The majority of these items were exported via Safi, where local weavers copied the patterns from samples of the desirable Oran and Tunis cloaks. Another North African cloth which was eagerly sought in the south was of white wool, which was manufactured in different patterns and seems to have been traded primarily through Arguim from Safi. It has been recorded that between 1500 and 1530, *lambens* were sold at Sao Jorge da Mina in the Guinea gulf at an annual rate of 2,500 to 3,300, while demand for *aljaravias* reached 4,000 at the height of their popularity (Vogt 1975:642).

Cloths with distinctive patterns were produced on the Cape Verde Islands during the period of Portuguese domination in the fifteenth and sixteenth centuries. The composition of the cloths, with their emphasis on overall surface decoration in repeating patterns, and the individual design elements, suggest inspiration from Moorish Spain and indirectly from North African textiles. L:202 cm; W:114 cm. 1934,3–7.195.

However, an unstable political situation in the Maghrib affected this expanding market and supplies of North African cloth rapidly decreased around 1530. The Portuguese had been challenged for control of the southern Moroccan trade by Genoese and Spanish merchants since about 1505. The strategically important town of Sus – located as it was on a gold route – was selected as a base for the Sa'dian leader al-Qa'im. The Genoese and Spanish merchants engaged with al-Qa'im in a mutually profitable trade, exchanging firearms, copper, and iron for local goods. Later, the production of sugar increased the prominence of this town, becoming its most important export. The final blow to the Portuguese control of trade came in 1541 when Muhammad al-Shaikh, a son of al-Qa'im, captured Agadir. The Iberians were obliged to withdraw from Safi during the same year, as the cost of maintaining this trade centre escalated.

Textiles from a different source formed the basis of another trading venture instigated by the Portuguese during their period of domination along the Guinea coast. Distinctive cloths woven on the Cape Verde islands and later in Guinea Bissau were manufactured with the intention of usurping, and thereby gaining control of, the local textile currency. During the fifteenth century the Cape Verde islands were colonised by the Portuguese who enslaved Wolof and Mandinka weavers from the mainland, and later developed for themselves a cotton weaving industry. It seems likely that the colonists brought with them cloth samples or patterns from Europe, which the indigenous African weavers were encouraged to imitate. The motifs used, relying heavily on diamonds, chevrons and the eight-pointed star, formed part of the standard repertoire of design elements on Hispano-Moresque textiles. These in turn were probably inspired by elements of Berber design, or forms from the Near East which the invading Arabs of the seventh century introduced into North Africa. Although woven in narrow strips, the choice of pattern elements, their repetitive composition and overall surface coverage, indicate Moorish inspiration. Their popularity on the coast serves as a lasting tribute to their enduring charm and appeal.

Thus, historically, North African textiles may be seen to have attained social, political and economic value through their significance as official gifts and items of trade, and by their prominence at life-cycle ceremonies.

2

FOOD OF THE LOOM
RAW MATERIALS
AND TECHNOLOGY

In North Africa, as in the rest of the continent, both natural and synthetic milled yarn has become widely available during the twentieth century. However, the range and distribution of locally produced fibres used in the manufacture of the handmade textiles of the region have not changed greatly over the centuries, and still broadly influence the geographical pattern of textile production. Wool, sometimes combined with goat or camel hair, is the predominant material used by weavers in the mountainous areas of the Maghrib countries to the west, whereas cotton, extensively grown along the Nile and Awash river valleys, is the basis of much of the textile production of Egypt, Sudan and Ethiopia. This is not to say that in certain areas, such as northern Sudan, the two materials may not be of almost equal importance, but there they are woven into different varieties of cloth, by different weavers, using different types of loom.

Wool and Animal Hair

Wool, particularly white, undyed wool, is widely believed to be a powerful substance which, when correctly used, may be prophylactic against a range of evil powers and influences. In Tunisia, if a young bride spun wool on the seventh day of her wedding, her marriage would be 'protected by the wool' (Poinssot and Revault 1957:25, Reswick 1981:58). In the Atlas mountains of Morocco, a tuft of wool worn in a girl's hair is considered to be an effective talisman, while threads of wool tied around the legs of livestock bestow *baraka* (blessing) upon them, and protect them from the evil eye (Sefrioui 1980:75). Similarly, a tuft of wool is often left on the back of male sheep in Tunisia at

Freshly dyed, woollen yarn strung
across a street of the dyer's market in
Marrakesh, Morocco.
Photo: R. Balsom.

27

shearing time, in the belief that this will protect the animal and its ability to mate (Renon 1944:107, Reswick 1981:56). Shearing is a male activity, but thereafter the preparation, spinning and weaving of wool is largely in the female domain, though, inevitably, there are exceptions. In Upper Egypt, for example, spinning was noted as being largely practised by men in the early twentieth century (Blackman 1927:162–3), and is still an exclusively male activity in particular areas such as Farafra Oasis in the Western Desert of Egypt. However, in recent years spinning in Egypt has become a predominantly female activity, in conformity with the rest of the region.

Washing is always the first step in the preparation of wool, whether it be in a clear stream of the High Atlas mountains of Morocco, in the salty shallows of the Mediterranean around Jerba Island, Tunisia, or in the waters of the Nile in Egypt and Sudan. Regional variations in this process are, however, of considerable interest. Among the Ayt Hadiddu of the eastern High Atlas of Morocco, Bynon noted that wool was washed by being soaked in cold water, beaten on a stone with a heavy wooden club to emulsify the fat, rinsed in the cold waters of a stream, then kept in the dark for several days, during which time it was believed to swell due to the *baraka* which it contains (Picton and Mack 1989:24). Wool washed and beaten in a similar way, but in the sea water off Jerba, was then sometimes immersed in a plaster solution before being removed and dried. When the wool was rubbed between the fingers, the dry plaster would flake away, taking with it some of the excess grease remaining in the fibres (Combes 1945:293–4, Reswick 1981:58). A third variation of the washing process, observed in the early 1920s at Omdurman, Sudan, is described by Crowfoot (1921:24):

Her method is excellent – she washes the wool in river water without any soap, dries it on a bed of clean sand in the sun, tearing it all the time, and then rolls it lightly in her hands. The result is a perfect 'rolag' (Scoticé) for spinning. The wool is clean but with the natural grease still in it, and the quick drying has prevented any shrinking or felting.

Once washed, the wool is sorted, then combed, using two implements with large metal teeth, in order to separate the longer, tougher fibres from which the warp elements of cloth will be spun. Sometimes goat or camel hair may be added to the wool at this stage to give it extra durability (Reswick 1981:58). Yarn for the weft of a cloth is obtained from carefully selected fleeces. It is composed of shorter and softer fibres which are prepared for spinning by 'carding', during which the wool is passed from one to the other of a pair of hairbrush-like devices set with numerous hooked metal 'bristles'. The longer fibres of the warp yarn are spun using a distaff and small, drop-spindle, its whorl pointing downwards. The spinning of the shorter weft fibres, by contrast, is accomplished using no distaff and a much longer spindle, one end resting on the ground or on a plate which allows it to spin freely (Reswick 1981:58). However, it should be noted that in some areas, such as northern Sudan, only short-stapled wool is widely available and that the differentiation noted above does not apply. Crowfoot observed that the spinning of wool in Sudan was accomplished with a single spindle, held with whorl uppermost (1921:24).

The complex process of turning fleece and hair into yarn, a process which at every stage is surrounded by ritual preparations and local beliefs, is here presented in a highly simplified version. Although the operation is broadly similar throughout the region, there is a great variation in local techniques, accessories and associated preparations.

Cotton and other plant fibres

Much of the cotton yarn used by contemporary hand-loom weavers in North Africa is machine-spun, and either imported or milled from locally cultivated varieties. However, in parts of the Nile valley and particularly in Ethiopia, the craft of preparing and spinning raw cotton by hand is still widely practised, and is evidently of considerable antiquity, though much work is still to be done in order to establish a clearer historical picture of the cultivation of cotton in Africa.

There are several species of cotton plant (genus Gossypium) now considered to be indigenous to Africa, two of which (Stocksii and Somalense) are cultivated in Ethiopia (Desta 1957:90) and produce the strong but very fine yarn, *tet*, from which the distinctive, muslin-like cloth of the region is woven (Donovan 1973:38). There are three distinct stages in the transformation of the freshly picked 'bolls' – the woolly balls of fibre which surround the seeds of the cotton plant – into ready-to-weave yarn: ginning, bowing and spinning. The process, as performed in Shawa province, Ethiopia, is described in detail in a mid-nineteenth century account (Johnston 1844 vol. 2:162, 321–2), and it is informative to compare this with more recent accounts of the same process in Sudan (Crowfoot 1924:83–9) and Nigeria (Picton and Mack 1989:30–32). As in the case of the preparation of woollen yarn, the comparison shows that the process remains broadly similar from one area of Africa to another, though the small regional variations are of considerable interest. It is worth quoting Johnston's account in full, as it accurately describes the essence of the process which is still carried out in parts of rural Ethiopia today. He begins by describing the ginning of the raw cotton (1844 vol. 2:321–2):

Flat stones, something larger than bricks, with a smooth upper surface, were placed upon the ground, my three factory girls kneeling down before them, each with an iron rod in her hands, about twelve inches long, and three quarters of an inch in the middle, and tapering to the extremities. This instrument is called a *medamager* [*madamacha*]; and with it a small quantity of seeded tufts of cotton, being laid upon the near end of the stone, is rolled out; the seeds, by the pressure being forced before the *medamager*, until they fall over the farther extremity of the stone. By this simple, but very effectual process a large portion of the cotton was soon in a state fit to be farther cleaned from dust and other extraneous matter, and which is the next part of the process it has to be submitted to before it is in a fit condition to be spun into thread.

Johnston then goes on to describe the process of bowing the cotton (1844 vol. 2:322):

The instrument employed for this purpose is called *duggar* [*dagan*], and is a large bow, the extremities of which are connected by a strong line of catgut. The cotton to be operated upon is placed in a clean soft hide spread upon the floor, whilst a woman, kneeling, holds the bow in the left hand over the cotton, so that the string is just high enough to catch the topmost fibres, whilst with the other hand, in which she holds the smooth curved neck of a gourd-shell, she continually keeps twanging away, each vibration of the string scattering and throwing up quantities of the lighter filaments, whilst all heavier matter sinks, as if in a fluid, to the bottom. The finer

Women of the Ayt Yazza of the eastern High Atlas, Morocco, spinning and carding wool in a tent at sheep-shearing time. The woman on the right is carding the wool which is being spun into coarse yarn by the woman on the left. This yarn will later be plied into cord which is used to bind the feet of the sheep while they are being sheared. *Photo: J. Bynon.*

portions, upon the summit of the heap, as it appears satisfactory, is taken off, and placed carefully in a large covered basket made of mat . . . The beautifully white dressed material is then taken out of the basket and piped, by portions being twined around the *medamager*, which being withdrawn, leaves a twisted lock. These, in numbers of six or seven, are folded together into a single knot, and laid by in a clean skin bag until they are required for spinning into thread.

Finally, Johnston observes two women spinning (1844 vol. 2:162):

The right thighs of each were completely bare to the hips, for the purpose of rolling swiftly with the palm of the hand, along the smooth surface, the small light reel, which hung revolving, whilst the hand bearing aloft the light white cloud slowly diverged to arms' length, and the other as gradually drew out in the opposite direction the slender thread that was formed during the operation.

Spinning was a craft learned by a large proportion of Ethiopian women throughout the social spectrum and, together with embroidery (see Chapter 7), was considered to be a fashionable and appropriate pursuit for noblewomen well into the twentieth century (Pankhurst 1964:223).

Crowfoot (1924:84) observed that Sudanese women, in an interesting variation on the procedures described above, preferred, if possible, to spin straight from the boll, and to dispense with any of the preliminaries:

The native bamboo hand gin serves their purpose better, but even that is not highly thought of. When the Sudanese expert spins she gently removes the lint from the seed, takes the soft fluffs two or three together, and with a few quick touches the light roll is ready. Scutching, carding or other preliminary processes are unnecessary – the essential ones, drawing, twisting, winding are all done on the spindle. Thread so spun has peculiar durability as the fibres lie much in their original order, and is soft with the softness of the cotton in the boll.

In antiquity, plants such as flax were much more widely cultivated in North Africa than they are today, and provided the raw material, in the form of linen, for the vigorous weaving industry of ancient Egypt. Before the Second World War, the remains of a once thriving flax growing and hand-weaving industry survived in the Cape Bon area of Tunisia (Gallotti 1939:758), though today the cultivation of the plant is mainly confined to the Nile Delta, the crop being processed into milled yarn for the production of machine-woven cloth. Other plant fibres used on hand-looms within the region include dwarf palm, esparto grass and rush, all of which are occasionally included in Berber tent fabrics and mats from central Morocco (Forelli and Harries 1977:47).

Silk and Synthetic Fibres

Silk was once locally produced in Tunisia, but nowhere else in North Africa, as attested by Ibn Hawkal's tenth-century description of the town of Gabes: 'It has markets within its walls, and great supplies of wool, besides which a great deal of silk is made there'. An anonymous account of the same region, which is based on the work of the eleventh-century geographer al-Bakri, substantiates Ibn Hawkal's observations (Serjeant 1951:44): 'There are many mulberry trees there, and silk is raised. This is the best and finest silk, none being made in Ifrikiya except here.'

It is not known when the local production ceased, but as in many other North African towns, raw silk was imported in large quantities into Tunis and Gabes, where it was cleaned, carded and spun by local women, before being used in a hand-loom weaving industry which flourished at least until the 1920s (Gallotti 1939:760), making a range of fine cloths such as the veils, 'ajar, which were worn by well-to-do women when seen in public. Silk was widely used in urban centres from Morocco to Ethiopia in the production of fine, flat-woven textiles, and is also the favoured material for the manufacture of belts and other narrow garments which are tablet-woven in Fes and in other towns of North Africa, usually by Jewish craftsmen. In a historical context, imported raw Chinese silk was locally spun into thick yarn before being tablet-woven into enormous altar-cloths, wall-hangings and other drapes to decorate the interiors of churches at Gondar in Ethiopia. Silk was also widely used in embroidery.

During the twentieth century, machine-spun yarns and synthetic fibres became more readily available to both urban and rural weavers. Rayon, for example, has now almost entirely replaced the silk once used in the weaving of cloth in towns like Naqada in Upper Egypt, and in the embroidery of a range of garments from places as diverse as highland Ethiopia and Siwa Oasis in the

A woman from the northern highlands of Ethiopia, spinning cotton yarn in the mid-nineteenth century. From S.F.F. Veitch, *Views in Central Abyssinia*, London, 1868.

Western Desert of Egypt. Lurex, which in recent years has been all the rage among Nigerian weavers, has also begun to appear in the hand-woven textiles of North Africa, particularly those of Upper Egypt, the supplementary weft patterns of which bear a striking resemblance to certain motifs commonly used by Yoruba weavers.

Dyes

The dyeing of yarn in North Africa is undertaken by professional dyers in the large towns and by the individual weavers in rural areas. The gradual introduction of aniline dyes since the mid-nineteenth century, and the wider availability of factory-dyed and milled yarn, has had a material and technical effect upon the trade, but the actual division of labour has remained virtually unchanged for many centuries. Al-Bakri, writing in the eleventh century, noted that the town of Fes in Morocco was an important dyeing centre, and that the work was done mainly by Jewish craftsmen. The fourteenth-century geographer al-Tijani (Serjeant 1951:45) describes the dyers' market in the town of Tawzar, west of Gabes (Tunisia):

Those of the inhabitants who exercise the profession of dyers, come there to spread out garments of various colours and embroidered stuffs. The eye of the visitor seems to see in front of him, a rich flower-bed, where flowers of a thousand colours blossom on the edges of fresh and limpid streams.

Gallotti (1939:749–51) describes the preparation of a range of natural dyestuffs in North Africa, including indigo. However, it is not clear that he has fully understood the process of reducing indigo to a colourless, soluble form in which it penetrates the fibres of the yarn. The dye subsequently oxidises into an insoluble form when the yarn is hung up in the open air to dry. Only then does it take on its characteristic, deep blue colour. Nonetheless, the description does provide an interesting picture of the workshop of a professional dyer in urban Morocco:

The equipment of a dyer's workshop in Morocco consists of two or three fireplaces of clay and brick, fitted with large earthenware or copper cauldrons respectively: furthermore a hand-mill consisting of two flat stones, a mortar for pounding dyes, sticks for stirring the dye and wringing the thread, and finally long poles suspended from the ceiling for drying the dyed silks and wools. For blue dyeing indigo is used, which has been brought to Morocco in English ships since the 18th century. [Indigo was also grown locally in Morocco (Serjeant 1951:51)]. It is sold in lumps and ground to a fine powder in the hand-mill. This powder is poured into the built-in cauldron of the furnace until the water turns dark blue in colour; to this are added two handfuls of dried figs, dates, or sugar, without any other mordant, [these ingredients are not in fact mordants, but assist in the fermentation process] and also a quantity of lye. The mixture is then allowed to ferment; this state is advertised by a distinctive smell, to recognise which is the sign of a good dyer. Before the actual process of dyeing, the bath is slightly warmed. The strands of wool or silk are first soaked in clean water, and wrung out; then they are dipped into the bath, and stirred about to ensure the penetration of the dye. According to the strength of the solution and the shade of blue desired, the time of immersion varies from five or six seconds to three or four hours. Throughout the process the temperature of the bath must be such as to allow the hand to be dipped into it without having the sensation of burning. After dyeing, the strands are wrung out, rinsed in cold water and dried.

By 1850 the professional dyers of Marrakesh (Morocco) were using aniline dyes (Park 1980:47), and yarn dyed in this way was used almost exclusively in certain rural areas by the 1930s, supplanting the natural, local dyes – and the ritual preparations which invariably accompanied the process. Unlike the relatively controlled and measured conditions under which natural dyes were prepared by professionals in an urban environment, the results achieved by rural weavers were inevitably more variable and unpredictable. We cannot begin to record the enormous variety of natural dyes available to the weaver in North Africa or the processes required to extract them. However, simply to make a list (undoubtedly far from complete) of some of the materials known to produce various shades of yellow, should give some idea of the scale of the task: wold or wau (reseda luteola), spurge olive, euphorbium mulbina, curcuma, buckthorn, cotton (tamarix articulata) and onion skins, takkoumt and yellow almond leaves, cow urine, evergreen oak bark, and safflower (carthamus tinctorius). In Oudref (Tunisia) women address the following prayer to the woollen yarn before dyeing it (Reswick 1981:58): 'May Allah put you on the right way / He who opens all doors / drink what you have to drink / and rejoin your friends'.

The particular qualities of natural dyes, combined with government assistance for indigenous crafts and the demands of a changing and expanding market, have ensured that they continue to be widely used in certain areas of North Africa. Reswick (1981:58) reports that the use of natural dyes is a rarity in Tunisia, whereas Forelli and Harries (1977:49, 1980:32) show that a Zemmour weaver from central Morocco, whether working professionally in an urban environment or catering mainly for domestic needs in a rural community, exercises a wide choice in the types of yarn she chooses to weave. Some might be locally spun and dyed by herself, using both natural and synthetic dyes, others might be aniline-dyed, milled yarn purchased in the market.

Looms and Weaving Techniques

Looms of the region vary in sophistication, from the simple framework of metal on which Bedouin women of the Nile Delta weave knotted, woollen rugs, to the complex device, with four treadles and up to seven heddles, upon which

A Bedouin woman of Sharqiya province in the Nile Delta weaving a patterned rug on a rectangular frame made of iron water pipes. Some commentators (e.g. Picton and Mack 1989:45) would not consider this a true loom, as it does not incorporate a heddle or shedding device.
Photo: C. Spring.

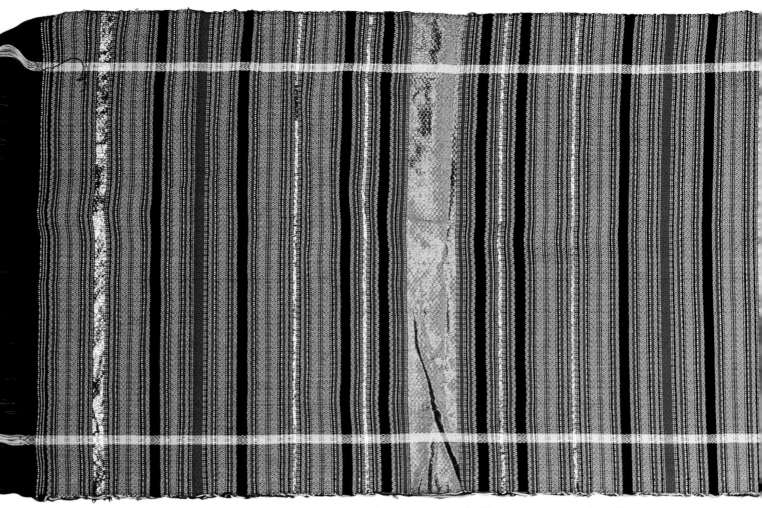

were woven the intricately patterned silk and cotton textiles of towns such as Fes in Morocco. Until very recently, it remained broadly true to say that woollen textiles of the region are woven by women on single-heddle ground and vertical looms, primarily for domestic use, whereas cotton and silk textiles are woven commercially by men using treadle looms. However, in line with the changes taking place in the hand-loom weaving industry elsewhere in Africa, the reasons for weaving cloth, together with the materials used and the division of labour, have altered significantly in North Africa during the second half of the twentieth century. It should also be emphasised that many of the materials normally associated with the treadle loom have long been in use on the vertical, single-heddle loom, and vice versa. Cotton yarn, both hand and machine spun, together with silk and rayon, are frequently used in the Berber textiles of central Morocco (Forelli and Harries 1977:47), and cotton provides the patterning on the woollen base cloth of the *bakhnuq*, *katfiya* and *ta'jira* of rural Tunisia. By contrast, fine, woollen cloth has been woven by men on treadle looms in the Nile valley of Egypt for many centuries, and is still woven by this means today in the Delta not far from Cairo. Among his various writings on the textile industry of Egypt, the eleventh-century chronicler Nasir-i-Khusraw described weaving in the town of Asyut (Serjeant 1948:109):

they weave cloth (dastar) of sheep wool, which has no equal in the world, and fine wools which are taken to Persia and which they call Misri, (Egyptian). All this is from Upper Egypt, for in Cairo itself they weave no wool. I myself have seen in Asyut a cloth (futa) manufactured of sheep's wool, the like of which I have not seen in Lahawar (Lahore), nor Multan, so that I thought it silk (harir) by the look of it.

34

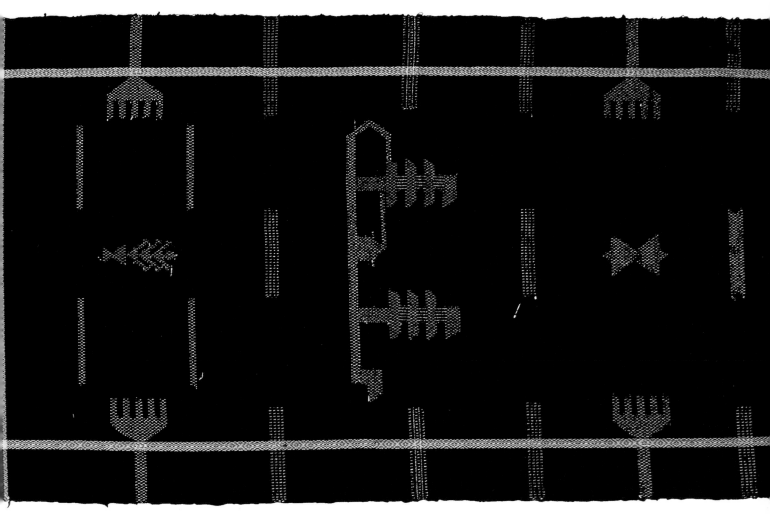

A cotton cloth with supplementary weft patterns in rayon and lurex. Such textiles are woven on small, treadle looms by women in the town of Naqada, in Upper Egypt, which has long been renowned for its silk weaving. Throughout Africa the treadle loom is normally used by male weavers. L: 386cm; W:54 cm. 1993,Af24.5.

THE GROUND LOOM

From Sudan to Morocco, the horizontally-disposed, single-heddle 'ground loom' is used in rural areas to weave tent cloths of wool (sometimes mixed with goat hair or vegetable fibre for extra strength), animal trappings, sturdy blankets and other utilitarian textiles. This type of loom, identical to those used in Palestine (Weir 1970:16–24) and elsewhere in the Middle East, is likely to have been transmitted to North Africa following the seventh-century Arab invasion. Changes in the life-style of many of the peoples of the region from a transhumant to a more sedentary pattern has inevitably led to a decline in demand for the products of the ground loom.

There are few regional variations in the structure of the loom, the main one being the way in which the heddle is supported, which may be by means of forked sticks or stones favoured in Upper Egypt and Sudan, or by a structure of sticks from which the heddle is suspended, as amongst the Berber peoples of the High Atlas mountains of Morocco (Picton and Mack 1989:57). Crowfoot (1921:26–8) provides a detailed description of a ground loom observed in Omdurman, Sudan. Bent (1900:337) describes a similar, but even simpler, loom used by the Bisharin of Upper Egypt and northern Sudan:

The yarn had been wound over two sticks about 20 feet apart, and that stick near which the weaving was begun was tied by two ropes, each a foot long, to pegs in the ground. The other was simply strained against two pegs. There was no attempt to separate the alternate threads so as to raise each in turn. There was a stick raised 4 or 5 inches on two forked sticks to separate the upper and under parts of this endless web of 40 feet. The weaver sat on her goat's hair web, and never could get the

35

Ground looms set up by women of the Ayt Yazza in the eastern High Atlas mountains of Morocco. The single heddle is suspended from a pair of poles joined together at the top. Such looms are used for weaving tent cloths. *Photo: J. Bynon.*

shuttle across all the way. It consisted of a thin uneven stick, over a foot long. She had to separate twelve or fifteen threads with her hand, and stick in a pointed peg about 10 inches long, while she put the shuttles through that far; then she beat it firm with this instrument and went on as before.

Murray (1935:61–2) adds this account of the use of a shed stick on a ground loom of the Bedouin of the Western Desert of Egypt:

When a plain piece of stuff such as a tent-roof is needed, a flat 'shedstick' *minshaz* resembling a broad wooden sword is passed between the warp-threads, the odd threads being evenly brought up and the even threads passed down. When the *minshaz* is in position holding the warp thread apart, the weft carried on a piece of wood is passed through. The *minshaz* is then pulled out and a gazelle horn is generally used to bring up the weft thread into position, and then again the weft is pressed home by the *minshaz* before it is used for a new line of weft. When it comes to weaving in patterns, the Arab woman carries the number of threads to be taken up or missed in her head – and this has been taught her in early childhood when she sat beside her mother weaving.

THE BERBER LOOM

More prestigious and intricately-patterned woollen cloths are woven by Berber women of the Maghrib on a vertically mounted, single-heddle loom of much greater antiquity within the region than the ground loom described above. Light and easy to assemble and carry from one place to another, the Berber loom is essentially the same as the ground loom, but raised into an upright position by means of two supporting poles, one on either side. Together with the warp beam running across the top, and the cloth beam along the bottom,

36

RIGHT An upright, single-heddle loom being used by a Shawiya woman from the village of Chebla, eastern Algeria, in the early twentieth century.
Photo: M. W. Hilton-Simpson, courtesy of the Royal Anthropological Institute.

A Berber tent set up among the ruins of Volubolis, near the town of Meknes, Morocco. The decorated side panels of such tents are often woven on an upright, single-heddle loom, whereas the strips sewn together to form the main body of the tent are produced on a ground loom.
Photo: R. Balsom.

these poles form a rectangular frame which is the essential structure of the loom. It could easily be set up within a Berber tent, the two uprights being secured to the poles which support the ridge beam (Forelli and Harries 1980:30). Here it might be used to weave the decorated panels, the 'walls' of the tent, which are combined with longer, ground-loom woven strips, *flij*, which form the 'roof'. Alternatively, and nowadays ever more frequently, it is set up close to a wall in a permanent dwelling.

Before weaving can commence, the warp must be arranged or 'laid' in a particular pattern which separates the two sets of elements which, when mounted on the loom, will provide the shed and counter-shed through which the weft will pass. This is achieved by winding the warp yarn in a figure of eight pattern around three pegs hammered into the ground, the length between the two outer pegs being slightly more than the length of cloth to be woven (Picton and Mack 1989:59). The warp must then be carefully transferred to the loom, with strict attention being paid to maintaining the correct spacing and tension of the individual elements. Finally, one set of warps is leashed to a single heddle rod which is pulled back towards the wall where it is permanently fixed. The weaver sits 'behind' the loom, with the wall at her back, the warp threads before her, and the heddle rod at approximately eye level. She may now create shed and counter-shed by raising or lowering a shed stick inserted between the warps above the heddle rod (Forelli and Harries 1977:50–52).

Every stage in the preparation of the yarn and the assembly of the loom, of which only a brief summary is provided above, is surrounded with ritualised acts to ensure success and to ward off evil. Once set up in this way, the loom and the textile mounted on it are recognised as a living being which experiences birth, youth, maturity, old age (Reswick 1981:60) and finally death, when the completed cloth is cut from the loom. Furthermore, the loom has a soul, which Messick (1987:212) identifies as being 'located at the moving crossing point of the two sets of warps.' Such is the power of the loom, that a range of events taking place in the community might be directly attributed to the weaving of the cloth.

THE TREADLE LOOM

In Ethiopia, the Nile valley and many of the large towns of North Africa, various types of horizontal treadle loom with two – and occasionally more – heddles, are widely used in the weaving of cotton, silk, and synthetic fibres. They are predominantly operated by male craftsmen. The main technical difference between the treadle loom and the single heddle varieties described above is that all, rather than half, the warp elements are leashed to the heddles. Instead of having to move a shed stick by hand, the weaver can create shed and

A 'pit loom' made of acacia wood being used near Rufa'a, Sudan, in 1985 to weave a cotton textile with weft stripes of blue rayon. The weaver sits on the edge of a hole in which his feet operate the treadles of the loom. He is beating in a 'pick' of rayon, the yarn being clearly visible in the shuttle boat in his left hand. *Photo: M. B. Spring.*

counter-shed simply by operating the treadles, leaving his hands entirely free to insert and beat down the weft. The mechanical principles of this type of loom are described in some detail by Picton and Mack (1989:45–53, 93–6).

There are numerous regional variations of the treadle loom in North Africa, though the basic mechanism remains the same. So-called 'pit looms' are widely used in Egypt, Sudan and Ethiopia, the weaver sitting on the edge of the pit above which the loom is mounted and in which he operates the treadles with his feet. Alternatively, the weaver may sit upright with his feet operating the treadles at ground level. Warp tension is normally maintained, particularly in the case of the pit loom, by passing the yarn around a post directly in front of the loom and just above ground level, then around a series of smaller stakes to the right, the skein being finally tied to a peg close to the weaver, allowing him to release more warp when required. Alternatively, the warps may pass through a pulley above the weaver, then down and under the warp beam in the front of the loom. This is the arrangement employed by the rag-work weavers of Cairo, who use a type of pit loom.

Perhaps the simplest types of treadle loom are the very small examples used in Upper Egypt and the Western Desert (Blackman 1927:163), and the tripod looms which Donne (1981:147–50) observed in use at Luxor in Upper Egypt. Both are designed to produce narrow strips of cloth which are used as decorative borders for larger textiles. Donne noted the similarities between these Egyptian looms and the treadle looms of West Africa, particularly the tripod loom used by the Mende of Sierra Leone.

At the other end of the spectrum, and also with West African parallels, are the large and complex 'draw looms' which were used in Fes (Morocco) for the manufacture of intricately patterned silk textiles (Lapanne-Joinville 1940: 21–65). Looms of this type acquired their name by being fitted with a number of supplementary heddles which would be 'drawn up', on the weaver's com-

A Muslim weaver in the town of Aksum, northern Ethiopia, using a double-heddle treadle loom to weave a *shamma* with a multicoloured border (*tibeb*). Numerous supplementary shed sticks have been inserted in the warp to replicate the complex pattern of the *tibeb*. *Photo: S. Bell.*

A belt with silk warp and cotton weft, woven on a draw-loom, probably in Fes, Morocco. The intricate pattern is influenced by French textile designs of the early eighteenth century. L:159 cm; w:40 cm. 1969,Af37.17.

mand, by one or more young boys (Gallotti 1939:748). Patterned cloth of Moroccan inspiration was woven in this way in southern Spain and Portugal during the period of the Hispano-Moresque civilisation, and it is likely that weavers fleeing from Christian persecution during the late fifteenth century brought this craft to Fes and other North African cities. As the Portuguese began to trade along the West African coast during the sixteenth century, it is thought that weavers among the slaves who were taken to the Cape Verde islands were taught the technique of weaving the complex patterns of these Hispano-Moresque textiles, a skill they brought with them when they were transported to Guinea Bissau. Today, weavers among the Manjaka and Papel of Guinea Bissau still produce complex patterns with the aid of numerous string heddles operated by young assistants, though they weave the narrow strips of cloth characteristic of the West African double-heddle loom. However, it is hard to deny the historical connection of the Manjaka looms with the draw looms of Fes and, ultimately, of both types with the looms of the Hispano-Moresque civilisation.

The device which made the draw loom obsolete was the automatic, selective shedding machine invented by Jean Marie Jacquard at the beginning of the nineteenth century. This device could be fitted to a hand-loom and was operated by a treadle, eliminating the need both for manual assistance in raising the supplementary heddles previously required for weaving textiles of complex pattern, and for memorising the exact sequence in which this had to be done in order to achieve the required pattern. It is likely that this device was, on occasion, used to produce some of the silk textiles of complex pattern produced in North Africa in the nineteenth and early twentieth centuries. Hand-looms with this modification were certainly used in recent years by weavers at Kerdassa, near Cairo (Lynch and Fahmy 1984:25).

Another innovation in weaving technology was John Kay's invention of the flying shuttle in the early eighteenth century. Instead of the slow process of passing the shuttle boat by hand through the shed, and the consequent limitation of the width of the cloth to the reach of the weaver (unless two weavers were involved), Kay's device allowed a single weaver, simply by pulling a cord, to catapult the shuttle through the shed along a track running beneath the warp threads. Hand-looms fitted with a flying shuttle were widely used in Egyptian towns of the Nile valley and Delta in the early twentieth century (Wells 1911:3–24), and may be found in a few weaving shops today. Here also it is still possible to see one of the means of preparing cotton and silk warp threads for mounting on the loom, a similar process being described by Lapanne-Joinville in Fes (Morocco) (1940:24–32) and by Weir (1970:27–30) in Gaza (Palestine) where the technique was said to have been imported from Egypt. The warp is 'laid' from two rows of approximately fifteen spools, one above the other, each spool being wound with machine-spun cotton and placed on a wooden peg which allows it to spin freely. The individual threads then pass through the teeth provided by two rows of nails, again one above the other, which keep them separate, then across two old neon light tubes which allow them to glide freely and prevent them from snagging. Finally they come together into a single skein which is wound onto a four-sided construction of wood, about eight feet high with a rotating central pole. The man operating this 'drum' skilfully keeps the skein separate as it is wound from the top to the bottom. Small pieces of bone are inserted beneath the skein after each revolu-

A tablet weaving loom from Tlemcen, northeast Algeria, pictured in the early twentieth century. Between the fixed, right-hand upright, to which the warp elements are hooked, and the moveable support about two thirds of the way along the loom which provides the necessary tension to the warps, the following accessories may be observed (right to left): a shuttle to which the weft thread is attached; a wooden knife for beating in the weft; a set of tablets strung on the warps; a comb to keep the warp elements separate. From A. Van Gennep, *Études d'Ethnographie Algérienne*, Paris, 1911.

tion to prevent slipping and mingling of the warps. Finally the skein is cut and wound into balls ready for mounting on the loom.

THE TABLET LOOM

Tablet weaving, in which the 'sheds' through which the weft passes are created not by heddles but by perforated cards strung on the warps, is practised in urban North Africa predominantly for the weaving of small, narrow garments such as belts. In Ethiopia, however, the weaving of much larger textiles on a tablet loom is well documented in a historical context (see Chapter 7).

The tablet loom as used in Morocco, Tunis (Collingwood 1982:38–53) and Algeria (Van Gennep 1911:68–82) consists of two wooden uprights, sometimes mounted on a flat base, between which the warp elements are stretched. Onto the warps are strung a series of square cards or 'tablets', each perforated with up to six holes through which the yarn passes. Patterns are created by rotating the cards, thus causing the warp threads to twist and form a shed through which the weft is passed. Variations in pattern and texture depend on the number of cards, how they are threaded and the method of rotation used by the weaver.

Tablet weaving is today mainly confined to towns of northern Morocco such as Fes where it is practised by male Jewish craftsmen, though historically it was more widely spread in the Maghrib and northern Egypt (Van Gennep 1911:79–80). A less sophisticated variant of the technique, in which the warps are stretched diagonally, and twisted without the help of cards, was still practised by women of rural Morocco in the mid-twentieth century (Chantreaux 1946:65–81).

Weaver working on a tablet loom in Fes, Morocco. He is threading individual warps between the teeth of the comb. *Photo: J. Powell.*

3

THE PATTERNS
OF LIFE

LEFT Detail from a cloth (*tanshifa*) used by Algerian women to cover the hair or shoulders. They were ceremonial pieces, reserved for use on occasions such as weddings, circumcisions or religious festivals. The bold foliate scrolls embroidered in purple silk are interspersed with Turkish-inspired flower patterns. L:282 cm; W:37 cm. 1907,10–16.11.

ABOVE Detail from a head-shawl from southern Tunisia. The embroidered motifs include the hand, fish and the eight-pointed star.
Photo: S. Paine.

The remarkable range of technical processes displayed on North African textiles bears witness to the impact of numerous foreign influences and the ability of the artisans to incorporate innovative techniques into their established repertoires. However, it is the motivation for the production of textiles and the power and function of the employed motifs in a local context which concern us here. While similar design elements and names may occur on textiles in town and rural areas, the inspiration for the continued use of particular patterns and the resulting overall composition of the pieces may be different; a reliance on popular religion, manifest in an adherence to ritual, folk beliefs and the spirit world, continues to dominate the patterns used on rural textiles. Patterns reflect community concerns, and individual creative impulses are to some extent governed by them. Weavers produce cloths – cloaks, shawls, bedding, tent panels and carrying sacks – which are essential in daily life and, accordingly, the motifs used are named after objects from the physical environment. Other cloths are produced for use at ceremonial or festive occasions; the patterns on these items may relay messages establishing their cultural function for a specific group at a particular time.

In urban areas there are different motivations: products may be made purely for sale, or pieces may be commissioned. Designs are frequently incorporated after the weaving process, so that cloth production and post-loom decoration may be executed by different people, rendering the relationship between cloth and producer less personal and less culturally definable. The complex mixture of external influences and associated peoples serves to stimulate innovation, while, at the same time, well-established motifs which provide an enduring social and cultural value may be retained and flourish.

Beliefs and practices associated with the concept of the 'evil eye' (*'ayn*) are well documented for North Africa and, indeed, encompass the entire Mediterranean area. The phenomenon was witnessed in ancient societies, and widely known prior to the spread of Islam. It is frequently linked to the notion of the

43

fear of envy, directed consciously or unconsciously by a living person. Patterns, motifs and objects have been described as prophylactic against the evil eye. Bynon (1984:140) expounds the theory that the prominent placement of certain objects, or patterns on objects, serves to attract the first glance of the evil eye. The possessor of the evil eye may be repelled or disgusted, or the eye may be symbolically pierced or attacked when confronted by these objects or motifs. The envious gaze may also be reflected back through the use of mirrors or associated symbols. In North Africa one of the most widespread means of countering the immediate impact of the evil eye is by use of the number five (*khamsa*). Throughout the region, images of hands are painted above doorways and windows, and on the boots of cars, in an attempt to avert misfortune. By means of spreading out the fingers of the hand towards the suspected carrier of the evil eye, or by pronouncing a formula containing the word *khamsa*, it is believed that the bad luck, illness or death that could result from an envious glance will be avoided. Patterns on textiles often assume the shape of a hand, or designs with five elements are incorporated as a means of protecting the wearer of the cloth, or the objects covered by the cloth, from the feared malicious influence of the evil eye. There are numerous other devices and motifs used in an attempt to combat this force, but descriptions of events connected with it and reactions to it are expressed in different ways according to region. The acceptance of orthodox religion and the dependence on God's will may provide comfort and strength in times of personal misfortune, economic failure, and social disorder. The evil eye concept may be seen as a popular means of rationalising misfortune within certain communities: it serves to protect people or their possessions from a perceived fear of envy. Rural inhabitants, especially, are keen participants in the process, possibly owing to their less active involvement in orthodox Islam.

The use of symbols customarily associated with protection against the evil eye in Sahel weaving villages (Tunisia), has been discussed by Teitelbaum (1976:63–74). In this area, workers who are divided from the main weaving group – either by operating outside the established workshops or by indulging in the illicit consumption of alcohol – are seen to transgress the bounds of appropriate social behaviour and to upset the economic balance. Controls regarding production rates, established by weavers working within the village workshops, are flouted in order to achieve greater personal wealth. The use of symbols locally associated with protection against the evil eye, such as fish-tails, believed to confer good fortune, are employed by both factions. The workshop weavers use them as a means of registering disapproval, thus providing a measure of security against the perceived malevolent forces of the 'outsiders'. Meanwhile, the workers breaking the output quotas also see them as a source of personal protection, enabling them to persist in their accelerated work rates; the fish symbols shield them from the interference of the workshop members.

The Rural Weaver and Designs

Women who weave enjoy an enhanced status in traditional rural communities in the Maghrib countries. The textiles they produce for their families are significant on a functional level by providing clothing, furnishings and gifts, as well as appealing in an aesthetic sense. Frequently, these cloths have integral design elements, so that the weaver is able to communicate her knowledge of established patterns, while selecting certain combinations to express an indi-

Geometric motifs from the back of a boy's hooded jacket, Ayt Ouaouzguit, Morocco. Similar patterns occur on other types of textiles, such as women's shawls and covers, as well as men's cloaks and shirts. They are also painted onto the outside of Berber houses by women. The diamond pattern, *tihuna*, apparently meaning 'small space', is also interpreted as a symbol meaning a single household. The design, when used on houses, may be seen as defensive, indicating protection and security. It is possible that the symbolism remains the same when used to decorate personal textiles. L:88 cm; w:84 cm. 1987,Af11.1.

vidual creative impulse. The use of patterns and their placement in woven textiles has been compared to the structure of poetry and songs. This link is succinctly described by Harries and Raamouch (1971:70):

. . . the novice weaver and the amateur singer approach their creative tasks with all the traditional patterns and units that they have encountered in daily use throughout their lives. The way in which they combine these materials and use the traditional patterns to create new compositions is a matter of individual talent and application.

Young girls learnt the art and technical skills of weaving from their mothers; this knowledge was transmitted within a well-established cultural tradition. The process of cloth manufacture itself was imbued with local beliefs, and girls would undergo various rituals prior to weaving, believed either to deflect evil influences or to promote positive creative powers. In Tunisia, before this knowledge was imparted, the young girl's suitability as a weaver would be tested (Poinssot and Revault 1957:42):

An egg was buried close to the tomb [of the local saint] on a Thursday or Friday evening and when dug up the next morning its appearance would reveal the girl's future. A white shell entitled her to weave plain blankets, black stripes indicated an aptitude for decorated textiles, and a shell reddened by clay suggested that the girl become a potter instead.

Weavers have been questioned as to their involvement in selecting certain patterns for their cloths; one woman recounted how, on losing her skills 'she returned to her familial home and slept near the tomb of the local saint. In the morning the patterns were restored' (Forelli and Harries 1977:54). In this case, the patterns taught in childhood are seen as part of an unconscious learning process: women are 'blessed' with this special knowledge, which is perfected through time and with practice.

Although many rural textiles may be seen as essentially functional objects, this view must be balanced by a recognition of the wealth of creative impulses in evidence and the impact of their social importance. As we have seen, weavers may enjoy high social status within their immediate group. The threads woven to produce textiles also serve social functions: creating and reinforcing bonds, providing gifts, delineating age, gender and marital groups, as well as supplying cloths used for ceremonial or ritual purposes.

Patterns on rural textiles in North Africa

The origin of the patterns used on rural textiles throughout the Maghrib remains obscure, owing to the movement of peoples and the dearth of surviving early textile examples. It has been suggested that weaving techniques in Tunisia were adopted from Tripolitanian people towards the end of the seventeenth century (Poinssot and Revault 1957:13). Yet, whatever the original source of inspiration, it is immediately evident that the basic design components used on textiles throughout this region have common identifying elements. These are used in varying combinations to produce textiles whose patterns have regional or tribal associations. Many of these pattern combinations have identical names; yet, throughout the Maghrib, motifs of similar composition may be given different names according to locality and function. This leads us to suppose that the importance of the patterns lies in their locally-assigned meaning and placement, rather than in any shared, articulated, representational value.

In rural areas, where life is regulated by the agricultural cycle, the inhabitants face harsh environmental conditions and diametrically opposed natural forces such as rain and sun, cold and heat. The names of the patterns employed on textiles suggest a predilection for physical comfort, protection and security.

The area of the Middle Atlas mountains (Morocco) inhabited on a seasonal basis by the Beni Mguild tribe is located on a plateau with a high annual rainfall. Traditionally a transhumant group, the Beni Mguild are well known as prolific producers of textiles, which display bold geometric patterns and employ distinctive colour combinations with white cotton contrasts. The motifs are based upon diamond or chevron shapes, arranged in horizontal registers. The names applied to these patterns may imbue them with a prophylactic function against the evil eye. Similarly, on Zemmour textiles the eye may be pierced symbolically through the use of named motifs such as sabre, lion's paw, saw or fibulae. Such names may also be viewed as defensive, in accordance with a harsh and unpredictable environment. In contrast, textiles produced in the isolated, protected and closely-knit Mozabite community (Algeria) may demonstrate through the names of their motifs a sense of harmony and settled domesticity. The *gandura*, a sleeveless tunic, is woven by women for their sons. The named motifs indicate a maternal concern for the protection, good fortune, wealth and fertility of the wearer: birds and their young, couscous grains, pomegranate seeds, the bride, a key (Parienti 1953:52).

Designs which are formed from the same repertoire of geometric elements and combined to produce distinctive patterns are also seen in Tunisia. The rural population gives its motifs names such as comb, jewel, lantern, bean,

LEFT Detail from the end of a belt (*hizam*) worn folded lengthways by Ayt Ouaouzguit women, Morocco. It is woven in the slit-tapestry technique with diamond, triangle and cross patterns predominating. L:234 cm; W:12 cm. 1969,Af37.11.

FAR LEFT A shawl used at marriage by women in Siwa Oasis, Egypt. The tiny embroidered patterns have been linked to solar motifs, and the choice of colours, predominantly red, orange and yellow are similarly associated with the sun. The hand design, probably performing a protective function, occurs throughout. L:134 cm; W:74 cm. 1991,Af11.4.

amulet and palm tree (Reswick 1981:62). The aggressiveness of some named Moroccan motifs is absent here; the naming may thus be seen to complement the lives of rural peoples, providing clues to the history of their modes of existence. In the mountainous region south of Gabes, Tunisian women are renowned for their finely-decorated wool and cotton shawls and shoulder cloths. These vary in composition from village to village, but are technically and decoratively homogeneous. The motifs include indications of their rural background with names such as 'hen's foot' and 'camel urine'; more interesting, perhaps, are the designs which provide a link with similar patterns

A woman's black shawl (*bakhnuq*) from the Gabes region, southern Tunisia, woven in wool and cotton and dyed after completion, revealing the white cotton motifs. It has been suggested that these designs resemble items of jewellery and the patterns of women's tattoos. L:214 cm; w:106 cm. 1973,Af28.6.

employed on pottery, jewellery and the designs painted onto women's bodies. The patterns provide both a means for women to express their artistic urges, and a way of placing themselves in the natural world, surrounding themselves with a body of similarly decorated tangible objects.

Widely scattered and occurring intermittently, though sharing an energy and spontaneity rarely seen on North African textiles, are cloths with distinctive hand-embroidered decoration in either wool or silk. Examples from Tunisia are frequently cited (Stone 1985: 125–31, Paine 1990: pl. 83, 106, 144). However, largely undocumented pieces of similar vigour appear in Libya and on textiles from Nubia. Tunisian examples invariably coincide with established centres of wool weaving, so that the embroidered motifs are added intentionally after this process. In southern Tunisia, the head-shawls used by women and girls in Gabes are distinguished by their extraordinary embroidered decoration, apparently executed by men, in strikingly bright-coloured thread. The rather crude geometric patterns and spindly human and animal figures worked in chain or herringbone stitch are schematic, pleasingly naïve patterns, which in form seem to suggest inspiration from sub-Saharan Africa. The patterns which emerge suggest birds, hands, the moon and palm trees: all motifs which occur repeatedly in the Tunisian decorative repertoire. However,

48

Detail from a gold-decorated marriage tunic from Monastir, Tunisia. Stylised fish forms are frequently incorporated into marriage costumes and represent one of the most ancient and enduringly popular good luck designs. Ceremonies involving fish form part of wedding festivities in Tunisia and are believed to promote fertility. L:111 cm; w:106 cm. 1991,Af4.1.

these embroideries are unique in their liberated approach. Further north, at El-Jem and Ksour el-Saf, embroidered motifs also occur, applied especially to garments associated with marriage. Shawls are imbued with symbols of protection and fertility such as the sun, moon and tree of life. These patterns recall ancient designs on stelae and tiles, and may be tantalising remnants of the expression of former beliefs and values. As such they may now be believed to hold some powerful but unidentifiable source of protection for the bride.

In Nubia, married Fedija women wore a black head-veil (*tarha*); some of these

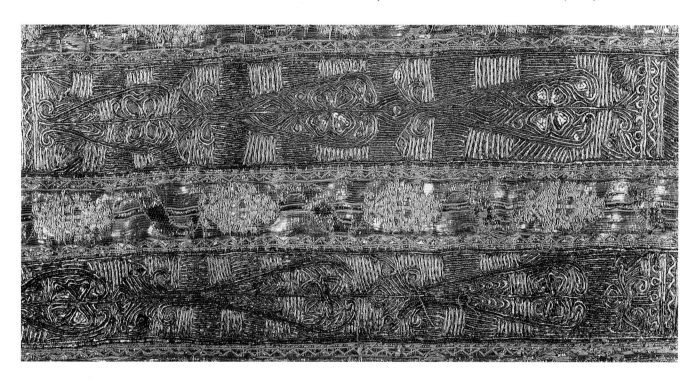

were decorated with brightly-coloured embroidered patterns. Women wore these head-veils when attending weddings and other ceremonial events. The geometric, representational and floral motifs in which birds and 'fleur-de-lis' patterns – which may be stylised palm trees – featured prominently, provided a lively and colourful contrast to their otherwise sombre clothing. Similar motifs also occurred when painted by women on houses. There may be a link between the meanings or patterns of these common motifs and their placement or context: patterns used on married women's homes and on their headscarves may indicate an expression of the desire for fertility. However, these patterns may simply reflect the women's wish to decorate their personal objects and homes with patterns which introduce colour and gaiety into a relatively featureless landscape.

OVERLEAF Front and back of a marriage waistcoat from Raf-Raf, Tunisia. Popular good luck motifs such as the fish, crescent, eight-pointed star and birds are embroidered in gold on a pink silk background. Male standing figures are also depicted. The waistcoats would have been worn under the marriage tunics, so these figures may be of purely personal inspiration. L:53 cm; w:61 cm. 1991,Af15.2.

Garments used by the bride during the wedding ceremony in Ghadames Oasis (Libya) are also decorated with silk embroidered motifs. These are strikingly similar to the cross-hatched floral and geometric designs painted in red onto the whitewashed walls of houses in preparation for marriage. Once again, the use of patterns such as the 'tree of life' may indicate a concern with protecting or promoting fertility.

Ghadames Oasis has well-established links with West Africa through the

settlement of a northern Nigerian Hausa-speaking group in the oasis. At marriage, Ghadames brides use Hausa cloths as part of their recognised wedding costume. It is therefore feasible that inspiration for the delightful embroidery patterns seen on their clothes and houses came via Hausa-speaking people. Male Hausa artisans continue to produce excellent embroidered designs on clothing today. David Heathcote (1976:15) suggests two possible sources of origin for this West African embroidery: one inspired by indigenous crafts imitating the designs used on gourds, leather, and pottery, together with the motifs seen on body decoration, the second based on more formal patterns adopted either from imported Middle Eastern cloths, or possibly embroidered in West Africa by foreign craftsmen. A collection of embroidery drawings by Alhaji Sanni of Kano (Nigeria) includes one intriguing design for a woman's blouse (Heathcote 1973:201). The linear, coloured decoration and the motifs employed – plant-pots, flowers, camels, birds and trefoils – are similar in both form and spirit to those seen on Nubian head-veils and the Libyan garments. The city of Kano in northern Nigeria enjoyed extensive trade links with North Africa and the Middle East; it is therefore tempting to suggest that inspiration for the North African embroideries was gained via these eclectic routes.

Embroidery patterns with a different emphasis occur on garments from the fishing village of Raf-Raf (Tunisia), which is well-known for its spectacular knee-length tunics. These are hand-embroidered by women with multi-coloured flower patterns, interspersed on the plastron (frontal panel) with popular Tunisian good-luck motifs such as fish, birds, moons, and the tree of life, as well as geometric patterns. The marriage tunic, of the same style, is extravagantly embroidered in wool and gold threads, the 'skirt' being liberally sprinkled with patterns recalling the designs painted onto women's hands at marriage.

Although certain design elements appear to dominate rural textiles, innovative motifs and patterns are experimented with and may gradually be incorporated into the basic repertoire, thus fulfilling a creative, social or personal need. In rural societies, well-established and accepted textile patterns are retained, thus creating a continuing link between mother and daughter, past and present. Newly devised patterns, however, will be accommodated, but only within the traditional framework, ensuring their smooth integration into the locally formulated repertoire. Harries (1973:151) writes: 'society seems to place great value on the skilled use of these traditional elements. Innovation is valued to the extent that it occurs within a traditional form.'

This rule-of-thumb may be transgressed, however, when economic hardship obliges women to produce textiles for sale. These commercially-inspired pieces of weaving, whether woven for use by town dwellers, or for a foreign market, may incorporate elements rarely seen on textiles intended for home consumption. Market forces emerge which distort the motivations inherent in the production of family textiles; the distance thus created allows a break with tradition and presents the weaver with the opportunity to experiment with a range of patterns outside her own daily experience.

Until recently, oasis dwellers in Egypt decorated their clothing with embroidered designs which were readily identifiable on a local basis. The significance of embroidery patterns on dresses from the Western Oases may lie in their placement on the garments. The patterns may provide functional, regional, protective or purely decorative meanings, or a combination of all these elements. The plastrons which cover the breast area are usually heavily embroidered, and further embellished with the incorporation of silver coins and, occasionally, mother-of-pearl buttons. In addition to their appeal on an aesthetic level, the latter materials may be seen to have a prophylactic value: both are shiny and reflective and may thus be used to attract the first glance of the evil eye or, alternatively, to blind it so that harm is averted. The embroidered frontal panels may also be protective in a more explicit way, by protecting the breasts which supply the infants' milk. The linear stitching running vertically down the body of the dress and horizontally along the sleeves may have a functional origin, providing a decorative means of strengthening or joining seams. Similarly, pottery from Siwa Oasis uses patterns believed to derive from the stitching on leather bottles – recalling a former nomadic existence. Today, these patterns are applied all round the vessel, having evolved as a decorative form, replacing an original functional status.

While both the black and the white dresses of Siwa Oasis used on the days following marriage may initially seem unique in their form and use of decoration, there are evident common elements between these dresses and those of other areas in North Africa. The T-shape is an ancient form, also seen today on tunics from Tunisia. Emanating from the frontal slit are multiple lines of embroidery forming a 'sun-burst' effect covering the front of the dress. The opening itself is surrounded by seven squares, each divided into eight triangular compartments. These patterns, by their position around the breast area and their use of the triangle motif, may be viewed as prophylactic; triangular shapes are used to decorate vulnerable areas on many items of clothing in North Africa, their pointed ends serving as defence against malevolent forces, while their overall shape recalls the pubic triangle, thereby indicating concerns about fertility. Mother-of-pearl buttons and, today, plastic amulets in the form of hands, fish, horns and even horseshoes, readily assert the notion of protection, for these are dresses worn initially by young, childless brides.

Patterns on Urban Textiles in the Maghrib

In urban areas, which have witnessed the greatest influx of peoples from abroad – invaders, settlers and immigrants – there has been a steady flow of innovative designs, which have engendered a fascinating melée of techniques, motifs, materials and artistry. Instead of persisting in the use of received and adopted cultural and artistic traditions, the people of urban North Africa have stimulated tradition by amalgamating some of these outside influences with the existing repertoire of patterns. The use of these varying designs on a range of objects, both functional and ceremonial, reflects a turbulent history, one influenced by Turkish, Andalusian, Middle Eastern and Mediterranean trends.

Patterns on textiles, as well as on leather, wood and metal objects and architectural elements, are distinguished by their overall surface repetition. The motifs for textiles fall into three main categories: geometric, floral and representational. As with rural textiles, the rhythm and balance of these motifs has been linked to an oral tradition. The custom of reciting verses from the Qur'an, together with the repetition of daily prayers, ablutions and invocations, may influence other quotidian activities (Sijelmassi 1986:35). The introduction of balanced, harmonious and recurring elements into woven textiles may be viewed as a natural extension of these pursuits.

Zemmour rug or saddle blanket from central Morocco, characterised by horizontal design bands separated by plain red stripes. The geometric patterns, based on the cross, lozenge, triangle and star, with some cross-hatching, are named and recognised locally. L:157 cm; w:100 cm. 1994,Af12.2.

Unburdened by arduous domestic chores, women and girls from wealthy urban families spent part of their leisure time embroidering textiles with colourful motifs in silk thread. They were initially instructed in this art by a *mu'allima*, a professional female embroidery teacher, who often owned a workshop. Girls from less fortunate families also learnt embroidery skills, and were recruited by these women as apprentices and employed to produce work for sale. Although women might experiment with new patterns, the range of motifs and the arrangement of selected designs used by the pupils were governed largely by the knowledge, skill and motivation of the assigned *mu'allima*. The completed pieces, whether household furnishings or costume items, were produced by women of varying backgrounds, either for personal use or as commercially viable products. In this way, knowledge of currently fashionable, or locally favoured, patterns permeated all levels of society, while economic factors intervened to reserve certain items for a privileged clientele.

In Algeria, wealthy women regularly visited the *hammam* (steam bath); an essential bathing accessory for fashionable women was the *baniqa*, a loose cap made of absorbent material, with long decorated ends used to wrap up damp hair after bathing. The embroidered lappets on these caps were dominated by large, restrained, foliate patterns, in red, blue or purple silk threads, interspersed with delicate flowers, often in pastel shades. Similarly decorated cloths (*tanshifa*), were worn at home, draped around the shoulders or covering the hair. These were reserved for use on special occasions such as weddings,

RIGHT The plastron of a velvet ceremonial costume from Rabat, Morocco. A cardboard template is overlaid with gold-covered silk thread to produce a stiff frontal panel. Amid the mass of floral and vegetal motifs are two hands, possibly acting as a protective device. L:50 cm; w:48 cm. 1969,Af4.3.

circumcisions or festivals. The scrolls and elaborate floral motifs were divided by horizontal lines of gold silk embroidery in geometric or highly stylised foliate patterns. The inspiration for the designs on both these items seems to have been heavily dependent on Turkish patterns; North African tastes were accommodated through the orderly and controlled use of individual design elements and an emphasis on repetition.

An even more rigid approach was adopted on embroideries made in Fes (Morocco), primarily for use as home furnishings. Many of these items were reserved for special occasions or used when entertaining guests. The rigidly composed geometric shapes were worked in monochrome, relieved only by stylised trees, plants and birds which enliven the borders. The geometric patterns echo ancient design motifs used throughout the Mediterranean, such as the tree of life, the eight-pointed star, the hand and the fleur-de-lis. In ancient times many of these symbols were believed to promote fertility or were used as protective devices; it is possible that they retain similar meanings here.

Some of the most visually distinctive embroideries came from the small town of Azemmour (Morocco). They were worked onto fairly narrow bands of white cloth and were used to adorn cushions, curtains, and the bottoms of mattress covers. The patterns suggest direct inspiration from Renaissance Italy and Spain; however, these elements may in turn have derived from motifs or legends prevalent in the Mediterranean area for centuries. Azemmour was under Portuguese rule from 1513 until 1541, while its neighbour Mazagan was held by the Portuguese for a longer period from 1502 until 1769. Refugees from Spain arrived and settled in the town after the fall of Granada in 1492 and there was a second influx in 1610. The spread of these diverse sources of inspiration is difficult to identify precisely; thus, one of the most surprising factors, given this complicated borrowing system, is that there remain identifiable regional and local styles. One of the most enduring patterns on the Azemmour panels was that of a vase flanked by two birds; in contrast to Christian theology in which doves were depicted, the Moroccan version favoured peacocks. Azemmour work also regularly represented stylised female figures, wearing full skirts and with raised arms. These recall depictions of ancient goddesses, frequently associated with fertility; in North Africa similar representations are seen on Phoenician carvings on Carthaginian stelae.

In contrast to the textile patterns seen in rural areas, where family-produced cloths are the norm, in the towns motifs are introduced in accordance with the personal demands of the customer. Owing to the diversity of such individual requirements, and the ready availability of external inspirations, selection may be made from a larger corpus of pattern elements. Aesthetic expectations may also differ from town to country; urban artisans may be obliged to replicate popular designs, and a technically accomplished piece of work may prove more acceptable than a textile exhibiting individual creative flair.

During the nineteenth century, continuing into the early twentieth century, elite Tunisian women wore beautifully woven silk head-veils ('ajar) when leaving the seclusion of their homes. These were originally produced in the village of Testour by refugees from Andalusia. Later, they were manufactured in workshops in Tunis, where one family by the name of Gammoudi gained a significant reputation; some of the pieces woven by the Gammoudi family were signed. The veils were decorated with repeating horizontal bands, separated by a central, transparent, black section, through which the wearer could see.

The textiles skilfully combined widely-used geometric designs, such as the cross, lozenge, star, crescent, and triangle with stylised versions of trees, and the hand. In addition, floral patterns, which seem to suggest Turkish influence, were evident; these took the form of large, stylised carnations flanked by elaborately curling foliate forms. The resulting compositions, which included so many diverse sources of inspiration, were notable for their balance, harmony and individuality. The wealthy owners secured a textile which conferred prestige, while simultaneously offering physical protection through its form, and symbolic protection through the use of patterns and motifs which had a well-established prophylactic function.

The male equivalent of the female embroidery teacher was the *mu'allim*, who specialised in finely-woven silk cloths and belts; these items were similarly produced in workshops, by young male apprentices under the supervision of the owner. The finished pieces were sold to a wealthy clientele. The silk belts (*hizam*) woven by men in Morocco, and especially those produced in Fes, demonstrate the wide range of motif influences manifest on a single textile-type. Pattern variations, which occur both horizontally and vertically, are inspired by multiple external designs. Floral motifs such as the Persian-derived hyacinths, tulips and bouquets are placed next to asymmetrical teardrop-shaped palm branches, reminiscent of forms on Oriental carpets. Heraldic designs, shields, and repeating rows of architectural elements derived from wood and stone carving, draw heavily on Hispano-Moresque patterns. These diverse geometric and floral motifs are combined to form a finely balanced and ordered composition. The belt-ends frequently feature an eight-pointed star, combined with a stylised form of the hand; both these motifs are believed to have a prophylactic function in warding off the evil eye, their persistent placement in this vulnerable position substantiating the theory.

Costumes used for ceremonial or festive occasions may employ patterns worked in gold or silver threads or sequins. The nature of the context in which the costumes were used, as well as the placement of motifs, may prove to be of equal importance to the ascribed meanings of the patterns. In Tunisia, in the town of Moknine, the marriage tunic (*qamajja*), was decorated with a solidly-worked frontal panel in flat gold thread (*tal*). The motifs included the sun, snakes, fish and the hand, all considered prophylactic against the evil eye; their placement across the breast area may indicate further protection. The tunic used by the bride in Nabeul for the *jilwa* ceremony is interesting in its use of *barmaqli*, an open-work gold thread derived from Turkey. The local name for this tunic is *jibbat al-'ayn fil-'ayn*, (the tunic of the eye against the eye). It has been suggested that the holes in the gold-work resemble eyes, which may be seen to provide protection against the evil eye (Stone 1985:155).

Marriage costumes worn and embroidered by Jews in Tetouan (Morocco) are ornamented with motifs which provide a tantalising link with garments prepared as funerary shrouds. In their use of similar decorative devices, and the identical placement of the patterns on both male and female costumes, their motifs are important for the contexts in which they occur as well as their suggested meanings. The ceremonial jacket, forming part of the female costume, exhibits spiral patterns which are grouped in sets of three on either side of the front opening, and appear in a smaller version on the shoulders. This pattern, identically placed, is also seen on the third tunic of a woman's set of shrouds. On their wedding day, wealthy brides in Tetouan wore parts of these

LEFT Appliqué tent panel from Egypt. The central design features opposing lions with human faces, chained to the base of a stylised tree. Pairs of lions, often bearing swords, were carved into nineteenth-century Egyptian marriage chests and are seen painted above doorways in Egypt. Similar motifs were depicted on the facades of Nubian houses and placed above the lintels. L:260 cm; W:170 cm. 1979,Af10.1a.

RIGHT The tomb of a marabout (holy man), photographed during the 1930s in Kairouan, Tunisia. Representations of lions occur on stone, wood, metal and pottery and they are also celebrated in popular songs and folktales. Lions were painted above lintels or around the doorways of homes or tombs, where they were viewed as guardian figures. In the Cape Bon region they were described as the 'protectors of the hearth'. The portrayal of lions flanking a tree lends them a heraldic aspect. However, one might speculate that the associated idealised attributes of virility, strength and courage are rendered impotent by the chains binding them to the base of the tree. Stylised versions of the hand, denoting protection, are represented on the door. *Photo: Courtesy of the Royal Geographical Society, London.*

pre-prepared shrouds beneath their marriage costumes. Thus, the parallels between marriage and entry into a new cycle of life, and death and entry into the afterlife, are explicitly associated. Spiral patterns are frequently connected with infinity and the expression of a belief in the afterlife, and have been recorded as elements carved onto Moroccan tombstones (Bourilly and Laoust 1927:66). Motifs embroidered on the front of male shrouds, which feature distinctive 'sun discs' or 'wheel' patterns, accord with the designs on outer tunics worn by men on ceremonial occasions; apparently these tunics are also used by the groom at marriage (Ben-Ami 1989:35–6).

The ingenuity of North African patterns and their distinctive overall composition on a wide range of objects lies in the ability of the artisan to borrow, modify and incorporate stimulating elements from other cultures, while in the process giving them a North African flavour. Although these external components remain recognisable, they are formed within a framework that is essentially North African in composition, co-existing with indigenous elements and, at the same time, presenting local variations. Diverse and previously unlinked motifs are combined to form delightful and original works.

4

DISPLAY
AND MODESTY
TEXTILES FOR MARRIAGE

Ayt Ahmad bride (Morocco), swathed
in red veils and preceded by a young
boy who represents symbolically her
wish for male offspring. The bride's
fingers are entwined with wool
stained with henna.
Photo: M. Morin-Barde.

Wedding ceremonies address many
issues: status, wealth and prestige within a community; honour, beauty and
refinement; fertility and the creation and breaking of bonds. In different
communities throughout North Africa the balance between these issues will
receive greater or lesser emphasis. In the whole region costume plays a major
part in the celebrations, whether on account of the breathtaking splendour of
the clothing itself or because of its symbolic use, reinforcing and highlighting
fundamental aspects of life.

The ceremony of marriage in North Africa is one of the most significant acts
by which individuals change their social status. There is general recognition
and acceptance that the participating couple have attained a certain social
maturity, though on many occasions the girls, especially, may be very young.
In Muslim societies marriage is seen as the ideal adult state: single men and
women are felt to be inadequate and are viewed with suspicion. Only at
marriage are they incorporated fully into social and religious life. Marriage
partners may be chosen with economic or personal status in mind; there may
be a desire to cement existing familial bonds through marriages between kin, or
to pool economic assets through 'strategic' marriages. Bound in marriage,
women are also by implication bound to adopt and accept certain duties,
restrictions and patterns of behaviour. These changes may be encapsulated in
alterations in types of dress, or even in individual items of clothing or personal
adornment; such changes may be understood purely on a local level or may
enjoy widespread significance.

Parallels have been drawn with circumcision ceremonies which also provide
a means of transition, the pattern of events for circumcision corresponding
closely to that performed at marriage (Ammar 1954:116–124, Barclay 1964:242,
Kennedy 1978:158–61). The male child, for instance, may be addressed as
'bridegroom' ('aris) throughout the ceremony and in the Sudan the young boy
(aged between 3 and 10 years) would be dressed in a groom's costume on his
circumcision day (Barclay 1964:242). However, the boy may also adopt an item
of female garb during the 'dangerous' period preceding the operation. Ammar

ABOVE Loose-fitting white cotton shirt from Ghadames Oasis, Libya, worn by the bride at marriage. The bodice and wide sleeves are covered in multi-coloured silk or shiny synthetic material. It is embroidered in gold thread, with floral motifs around the bodice opening. L:109 cm; w:154 cm. 1981,Af5.9.

LEFT Detail from a shawl from the Ghoumerassene region, southern Tunisia, ingeniously woven in a combination of white cotton, white wool and black-tinted wool. When completed, shawls such as this were dyed red, black or indigo; as the cotton resisted the dye, only the white wool accepted the tint. The shawl above is plain and roughly cut at one end, suggesting that it is unfinished. It may have been intended to embroider designs at this end. L:133 cm; w:155 cm. 1973,Af28.7.

(1954:117), writing about a village in Egypt, comments that the boy wears a girl's brightly coloured headscarf, which is tied by the barber who will perform the operation with the words: 'let us put this female cloth around you, and by making you look like a girl tonight, you will be able to avert the evil eye'. Ammar suggests that this indicates a turning-point in the young boy's life, in that he now joins a clearly-defined gender-oriented social group and that anything connected with female attitude and dress must be discarded. However, young brides-to-be assume male clothing prior to the consummation of the marriage as protection against malevolent forces; this reverse-dressing may be both a means of averting evil glances and of protecting onlookers from polluting contact with the chief participant, who is regarded as both potent and vulnerable.

The differences between male and female clothing become most noticeable at puberty, small girls being provided with suitably 'concealing' clothes, boys wearing specifically masculine garments for the first time. At a relatively early age, more restrictions are placed on the dress and behaviour of girls than boys. At this stage, girls may begin to wear loose trousers, dresses with long sleeves and headscarves – so that even in play accusations about immodest behaviour cannot be levelled at their mothers. They may be restricted in physical movement, spatial movement, or both. As they grow older, they may be increasingly involved in female duties such as child-rearing, food production and water-fetching, which, in rural or lower-class households, centre on the home and enclosed courtyard. These deep-rooted concerns about modesty and honour are reflected in the extent of body cover adopted; however, analogous to this is an acute desire that girls will, nonetheless, be attractive to appropriate marriage partners. This dichotomy – retaining modesty while displaying

63

physical attractions – provides an interesting perspective when viewing dress as a means of communication.

In one context, women are identified as both weak and vulnerable, in need of male protection. Conversely, they may be perceived as a threat to male honour. Their newly-awakened sexual impulses are seen as potentially disruptive forces, with important implications for family and group life. In the tense period before marriage, the pressure on women to present an 'acceptable face' in public is ever-present.

Even where women are expected to wear modesty garments, they can successfully express individual characteristics and preferences. Clothing can be draped provocatively, revealing in a tantalising way the shape of the body, yet concealing the bodily flesh. Many modesty garments are made of shiny, fine or silky material which attracts as much as distracts the glances of prospective partners. Nubian girls can be seen in Aswan and around Kom Ombo wearing a version of the traditional black over-dress (*girgar*). This floor-length modesty garment, with a long train or deep ruffle was, in an older form, worn by Nubian Fedija women. It has been suggested (Mehrez 1993:1) that the ruffle was designed to remove all traces of the woman's footsteps as she walked. Interestingly, the Arabic verb *jarjara*, from which the name of this garment may derive, means to trail, drag or shuffle along. The innovative knee-length version seen around Aswan is made of semi-transparent material which reveals brightly coloured dresses below. The garment has become an attractive item of clothing in itself: the 'modesty code' is observed but skilfully manipulated. Winifred Blackman, who lived in Egypt during the 1920's and 1930's, noted that the normal attitudes to modesty might be suspended temporarily in order to secure a marriage partner. She commented that a young girl would be dressed in her finest clothes in order to attract a husband, her sole attempt at modesty being 'a veil drawn coquettishly across her face' (1927:43).

Wedding Preparations: 'something old, something new, something borrowed . . . '

Marriage celebrations create a particular need for specific items of clothing and other textiles. There are important distinctions to be drawn between newly acquired or produced textiles provided by either the bride's or groom's families, and borrowed or inherited cloth. The use of these items at marriage emphasises the role textiles play in creating relationships, weaving together individuals, families and generations.

In North Africa, the bride's trousseau, mainly consisting of furniture and other domestic items, personal clothing and jewellery, is accumulated in part with money from the marriage payment. One of the obligations of a man in North African society is to provide material support for his wife and children. By supplying gifts of clothing prior to marriage, either through traditional dowry stipulations, or as voluntary presents, he is able to demonstrate both his commitment to this duty and his willingness to accept his new role.

In the northern Sudan, the bride is provided with several complete outfits by the groom. It is anticipated that he will supply eight *thawb*, plus accessories and some negligées. He may also be expected to purchase a modern white wedding dress (Hall & Ismail 1981:156). Attitudes and practices have changed with regard to material provision. Traditionally, the groom in a Delta village in Egypt bought 'an iron bed and a wardrobe, the mattress cushions and covers were made from cotton. The bride got . . . dresses'; today, 'all men have to buy modern furniture and clothes for the bride' (Weyland 1993:161).

Among the requisite items provided (by the groom) for the bride's trousseau in rural southern Tunisia used to be a fine wool and cotton wedding shawl (*bakhnuq*); these shawls were woven by Berber women south of Gabes and around Tataouine. They were dyed red, blue or black, and decorated with designs woven in white cotton said to symbolise the bride's jewellery (Skhiri 1971:53). Today they are worn less frequently, but formerly, the different colours were used to mark significant stages in women's lives: young unmarried girls wore white, married women red and older women indigo or black shawls. The bride treasured items such as these, which incurred great financial outlay on the part of the groom and required months of labour on the part of the weaver.

Textiles and clothing from the bride's trousseau were her personal property, to dispose of at will. Today, in urban Tunisia, marriage tunics are extravagantly embroidered and elaborated with gold and silver thread, braid and sequins. Women in Tunis reportedly only sell these costumes in times of severe economic need; however, the motivation for this imperative varies throughout the country. Women in Sfax, eager to gain precious land in order to plant olive trees, will more readily sell their marriage tunics, and in Sousse the bride may sell her clothes and bed-coverings a mere seven days after the wedding.

In rural areas, the emphasis may be on finely woven woollen articles such as rugs, tent-cloths, bed-covers or wall-hangings. The items chosen match the patterns and emphases of life, and the choices made are determined by what is economically viable for the region in question. Gold and silver are more easily traded in an urban environment, whereas in physically harsher climes, 'luxurious' items include finely woven woollen textiles. All can be disposed of in times of need, thus providing a degree of financial security and independence for the women.

The groom may supply 'gifts' of clothing. Westermarck (1914:24) comments that on the afternoon of the *fatiha* ceremony – which involves the recitation of a prayer – the groom sends his fiancée new clothing; this is reciprocated when she sends him gifts of food on small tables. The tables are returned with a new article of clothing for the bride. In this instance, both parties are seen to have fulfilled their future duties: he has provided clothing, and the bride has engaged in food production, a task central to her new role. In some regions an itemised list may be requested as part of the marriage payment, whereby specific items, materials and quantities of clothing can be assured. During the nineteenth century, the marriage contract in Sfax stipulated certain items for the dowry, including a silver-embroidered tunic, a velvet caftan, and a face-veil, plus another veil embellished with gold coins, to be supplied prior to the consummation of the marriage. Thus, a considerable amount of personal 'property' was settled on the bride. In Tunisia today, the dowry is composed of two parts, one of which still specifies the provision of clothes and jewellery.

The groom's father may also participate in the buying process. In the small town of Yefren (Libya), he provides the bride's wedding dress, as well as special clothes for close female relatives and the groom. The bride's mother will receive a large woven cloth, a 'veil of milk' (*rida' al-halib*) which is given as a form of payment: compensation for the loss of her daughter and acknowledgement of a continuing link via the nurturing milk provided in infancy.

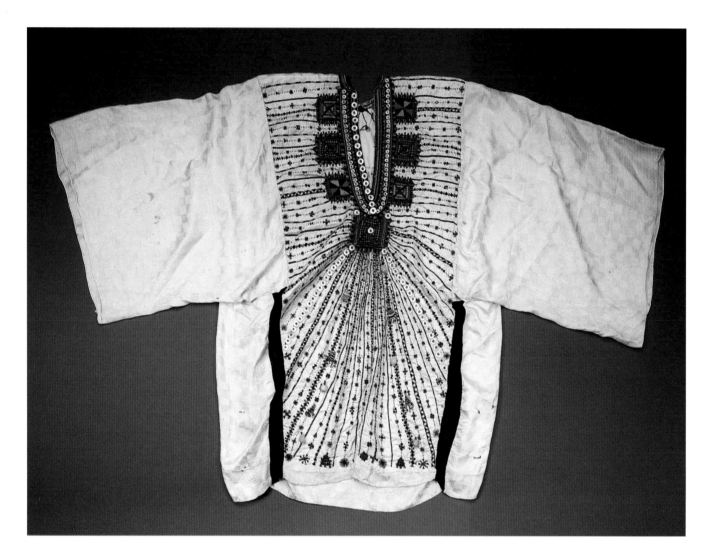

The *asherah nahuak* is worn on the third day of the wedding celebrations in Siwa Oasis, Egypt, when the bride receives her parents and family. The silk thread decoration is said to represent the colours of ripening dates. Throughout North Africa, dates are offered or received by wedding participants in an attempt to ensure the fertility of the bride and groom. In Siwa, dates are the major cash crop and thus also signify economic stability and wealth. Conversely, the red, yellow and orange threads may be associated with the colours of the sun. As Siwa has a well-documented link with the ancient Egyptian sun god Amun-Re, we might speculate on a continuing preoccupation with the sun in this use of colour. L:122 cm; w:184 cm. 1991,Af11.1.

Gifts of clothing may be reciprocal. Weiner and Schneider (1991:3) observe that 'many societies also assign women, rather than men, to exchange or give the cloths that tie . . . the bride's family to the groom's family . . . '. These unique opportunities for creating ties and obligations are organised and executed by women throughout North Africa, giving them a substantial degree of social influence. In Morocco, female members of the groom's family send presents, usually of clothes, to the bride at the *milak*, engagement party, (Geertz, Geertz and Rosen 1979:365). On the morning after the wedding day, the women of the bride's family carry gifts of clothing to the groom's house for both him and his family. In this way the two groups can be seen to have united through reciprocal gifts of clothing.

On approaching marriage, the bride and her female family members will often be busily engaged in producing items of clothing and textiles for use both at the marriage ceremony and afterwards in everyday life. The textiles in question will vary from region to region, and between rural and urban populations.

Among the nomads of southern Tunisia, the bride and her female relatives weave the red and white woollen belts she will wear after the seven days of the wedding festivities. By then she will have left her own kinship group and have

66

A nineteenth-century silk belt (*hizam*)
worn by Moroccan women on
ceremonial or festive occasions. The
design is composed of floral patterns
combined with heraldic motifs derived
from Hispano-Moresque architectural
elements. The base colour, dictated by
the ikat-dyed warp threads, graduates
from green to blue. Belts such as this
were produced on the draw-loom,
predominantly in Fes. L:231 cm;
w:17 cm. 1985,Af2.2.

moved or be in the process of moving to another, usually under the supervision of her mother-in-law. The belts produced will thus link her to her own female relatives in what may be a difficult and strange environment.

These continuing ties may be achieved in other ways. The women of Siwa Oasis (Egypt) continue to transmit knowledge of the designs and patterns on the richly decorated wedding clothes to their daughters (Bliss 1982:40). These clothes are produced in anticipation of marriage by young girls under the supervision and guidance of their mothers or other female relatives. Similarly, the women of Ghadames Oasis (Libya) embroider onto imported cloths floral and geometric designs related to those painted onto their houses; both are produced for marriage ceremonies by women.

Women of the Mzab (Algeria) weave a large piece of cloth, *jarbiya*, which is used to cover the bride and groom on their marriage night, both symbolically and physically uniting them. It is woven by female members of the bride's family from the date of her birth and at the death of the weavers continues in importance, becoming a tangible remembrance of them.

The gifts of textiles and jewellery supplied by the bride's family may be seen as gifts of affection, serving as links to her original family group. In urban areas where money may be donated or where clothing is heavily endowed with costly materials, financial security is provided.

Marriage costumes or parts of the costume may also be inherited. It has been asserted (Goldberg 1980:90) that among the Jews in Libya the groom would, by right, adopt a white cotton gown for the wedding ceremony instead of his customary ewe's wool robe; it would subsequently be stored away and inherited by his sons at their marriages.

In urban Tunisia, the gold-embroidered plastrons of wedding dresses may be removed, stored and then reused on a new dress. These embroidered dresses were costly not only on account of the rich materials employed, but also because of the number of skilled workers involved in their production. The wealthiest families would pay a specialist (usually Jewish) to embroider the designs; buttons and passementerie work might be completed by other artisans. By carefully preserving the garments in this way, the most expensive and finely woven piece of the costume would remain in the same family for generations, continuing artistic, aesthetic and personal traditions. Similarly, the women in the Western Oases of Egypt, Sinai and in Sharqiya Governorate, embroider and embellish the plastrons, hems and seams of their wedding dresses. Young girls are taught this art by their mothers, while preparing clothes for their wedding day. Finely executed plastrons may be cut out and incorporated into a new wedding dress when the original dress material has worn thin with age and wear. The wedding dresses themselves will be passed from mother to daughter. Thus, there is a continuing link between the young bride and her female relatives through the inheritance of clothes, patterns and techniques.

In Tunisian villages where marriages may still follow a formal traditional pattern, the wedding costume and jewellery is borrowed from a *mashita*, a woman who is employed to attend the bride during the wedding celebrations. She provides the jewellery and clothing and organises the musical entertainment. She may own a selection of complete costumes, varying in quality and price. Bayram (1977:9–10) writes of a *mashita* [*machta*], of one Sahel village who is reportedly in great demand, being engaged by families from neighbouring

This bride from the village of Ayt Iddir (Morocco) wears five veils in succession, secured by a chain of coins. The outer red veils completely cover her face and the elaborate form of the head-dress serves to disguise her shape and to protect her from envious glances.
Photo: M. Morin-Barde.

communities; such is her popularity, disputes often arise when her services are requested by more than one family for the same period. A *mashita* in this enviable position may become a very wealthy woman.

As costumes in the towns increase in cost, due to elaboration of decoration and the demand for luxury materials, many families are unable to cover the cost of new outfits for the marriage celebrations. They also may resort to borrowing costumes, either from women who have set up in business or from neighbouring families who possess these valuable articles. Women now produce fewer clothes at home and so families who have retained these costumes are able to profit repeatedly by hiring them to prospective brides. In urban Morocco, Jewish brides were given sumptuous wedding costumes by their fathers; as the cost of these outfits increased the custom was abandoned and, by the early twentieth century, women were obliged to borrow such items from their mothers and grandmothers.

The distinctive and elaborate marriage costumes of the Muslim brides from Fes (Morocco) are rarely purchased for the occasion; the cost would be too great. Thus they are hired, from a *naggafa*, a female specialist who may charge an exorbitant fee for the privilege. She will be in attendance throughout the ceremonies, to help pile on layer upon heavy layer of fine clothes: the greater the level of opulence, the greater the show of wealth and status within the community. The young brides are dressed and 'exhibited' for all to observe and examine.

Men also may borrow or rent clothing for the wedding ceremony, even in rural areas. The men of the Mzab (Algeria) wear silk and finely woven woollen items which would be expensive to purchase, so these articles are often borrowed for the occasion (Goichon 1927:89).

Individual items of clothing may be lent to the bride to bring good luck, fertility and happiness in her new life. In Bizerte (Tunisia) the bride borrowed the shirt she would wear on her wedding night – prior to consummation of her marriage – from a mature, married woman, the implication being that it had been used previously by a woman blessed with a long, happy and fruitful marriage. Married, childless women are reported to have lent wedding clothes to orphans who would otherwise not be able to bear the expense (Stone 1985:108). This being an act of charity in accordance with Islamic beliefs, it was to be hoped that the woman would subsequently bear children as a reward for her selfless act.

The Wedding Ceremony

Marriage ceremonies follow broadly similar lines throughout North Africa, though variations occur in the timing of events, the degree of elaboration, individual rituals, superstitions and the emphases placed on them. The central focus is 'the night of entering' (*lailat al-dukhla*), when the transition from childhood to adulthood is recognised; this may be the moment when the marriage is consummated, but in some areas, such as the Sudan, this event may take place at a later date, due to the severity of female circumcision.

Accounts of rural wedding ceremonies have tended to focus on 'ritual' events, the stages leading to *lailat al-dukhla* with the accompanying local superstitions and attempts to avert the evil eye. The differences are of emphasis: urban wedding descriptions have detailed the extravagance of the costume and jewellery of the bride, pointing to the importance placed on

On the evening of her wedding day the Tlemcen (Algeria) bride is presented formally to the assembled guests in a special ceremony called *jilwa*. She is dressed in a gold-embroidered caftan and silk robe. The scarf covering her face is removed and she stands motionless, with her arms at her sides and her eyes closed. It has been suggested that this posture may be designed to protect the resplendent bride from malevolent glances. From C. Ougougag-Kezzal, 'Le costume et la parure de la mariée à Tlemcen', *Libyca*, 1970, XVIII:255.

A Jewess from Tetouan, Morocco, wearing a version of the ceremonial costume, the *kiswat al-kabira*. This sumptuous velvet outfit was worn throughout the country, major towns developing their own distinctive cut, design and colour. The style of the delicate gold-work decorating the skirt-front is thought to have been influenced by Spanish forms. These were retained by Jews who initially settled in northern Moroccan towns, such as Tetouan and Tangier, after their expulsion from Spain. From O. Lenz, *Timbuktu. Reise durch Marokko, die Sahara und den Sudan*, Leipzig, 1892.

display and the recognition of status and prestige within the community; rural weddings follow formal timetables, where honour and status are achieved by correctly adhering to and observing set patterns of behaviour, and locally-held superstitions concerned with fertility are strictly observed. External influences may take longer to penetrate and are sometimes less easily accepted.

Rituals completed at marriage are performed only for those marrying for the first time. The symbolic importance of the event relies on this fact, because the ceremonies mark an important *rite de passage*, whereby individuals pass through various stages of preparation, transition, separation and graduation. The use of specially designated clothes during the wedding ceremonies serves primarily to highlight concerns about fertility. Until recently, rural wedding clothes in particular were frequently based on the shapes and designs of everyday dresses, but would be painstakingly embroidered or made from more expensive materials than ordinary dresses. In the Sudan, the essential female clothing item, the *thawb*, is retained at marriage; however, the customarily plain garment is decorated with shiny, metallic embroidery or sequins to render it 'special'. Sometimes this will be worn in conjunction with the modern white wedding dress. Clothes used throughout these stages reveal a way of thinking about fertility, relationships and status.

The days preceding the wedding day (*yawm al-dukhla*) present an excellent opportunity for the public display of goods purchased with both the marriage payment and contributions from the bride's family. In both rural and urban communities items of clothing, jewellery and furniture are paraded around the locality, inviting the admiring gaze of neighbours and relatives. In Sidi Ameur (Tunisia) a camel was customarily laden with the *ta'am* (food items) presented by the groom, and decorated with the petticoats, shawls and scarves he had also provided. Today, a car may be filled and embellished with these items (Abu Zahra 1982:129). Thus equipped, the bride's family and hired musicians parade around the village, exciting admiration at the splendour of the gifts and the generosity of the groom. This procession acknowledges the honour of the bride and her family and reaffirms their social status within the community.

The public display of goods is continued when female neighbours and relatives come to the bride's house to inspect and discuss the clothes and cosmetic items displayed there. The women of Ghadames Oasis (Libya) viewed the bride's trousseau at the groom's house, the dresses, shirts and outer robes being laid out for inspection on the groom's woollen cloak. In Nubia, among the Kenuz, the presentation and display of engagement gifts was undertaken in a special ceremony called *waddah*. The bride and female members of her family received gifts of clothing and cosmetics, meant to signify the recognition and acceptance of a new obligation on the groom's part. These items were initially displayed by the groom's mother for her neighbours and friends, thus establishing the wealth and generosity of her son, subsequently being carried in procession to the bride's house on large trays. The bride's family reciprocated by returning the trays piled high with cooked food: a gift for the groom. Sometimes the *waddah* gifts would signal a break with tradition, as Kenuz migrants in the towns and cities of Egypt brought home new styles of clothing to present to the bride and her female relatives.

In the village of Kafr el-Elow (Egypt), on the evening of the wedding (*lailat al-dukhla*), the domestic and personal items purchased with the marriage payment are displayed and examined, serving as a comment on both the wealth

A velvet wrap-around skirt from Rabat, Morocco. This formed part of the Jewish ceremonial outfit (*kiswat al-kabira*) and was worn with a short jacket and a plastron. The machine-produced gold braid-work which appears on this costume and other later examples may have been an inexpensive 'copy' of the luxurious and costly hand-embroidered earlier versions. L:102 cm; W:306 cm. 1969,Af4.1.

and prestige of the groom and his recognition of the honour of his bride. The gifts of clothing and jewellery painstakingly accumulated by the bride's mother in the years preceding the wedding are shown separately (Fakhouri 1972:68). The quantity and quality of clothing and domestic textiles play an important part in this female assessment.

In Tripoli (Libya), 'the day of turning' prior to the wedding day itself presents female members of the groom's family with the opportunity to view the bride. In some cases this will be the first time the groom's relatives have been able to observe the bride closely, as a marriage proposal does not necessarily imply familiarity with the bride herself. During the afternoon the bride, wearing her wedding costume, will be obliged to walk seven times round a basket of henna under the close scrutiny of the women present. Thus, the young woman is examined for physical defects and items from her trousseau are displayed. The red henna, symbolising the blood of the loss of virginity, demonstrates another essential attribute of the ideal bride.

In Egypt, the occasion of the bride's bath – an all female affair – may provide members of the groom's family with a similar chance to examine the bride. The guests join her in feasting, bathing and dressing in fine clothes. One of the most eagerly awaited parts of the celebration involves the display of the bride's amassed trousseau. This may include clothing items supplied by the groom as part of the marriage payment, as well as garments provided by her own family. These 'exhibitions' are an integral part of the wedding preparations and serve to establish the couple in an economic and social context.

The bride may be displayed formally to the groom, after a period of concealment following the official engagement declaration. Lane (1871 vol.1:217) cites such an instance for the wealthy citizens of Cairo in the nineteenth century: 'the bride is displayed before the bridegroom in different dresses, to the number of seven'. A similar ceremony in Siwa Oasis has also been noted by Fakhry (1973:57):

when the bride is dressed in the evening of her marriage day, she must wear seven garments one over the other. The first, which is next to the skin, must be white in colour and of a thin transparent cloth; the second is red and transparent also; the third must be black; the fourth is yellow; the fifth is blue; the sixth is of red silk and the seventh is of green silk. Over these she wears a special marriage dress, very richly embroidered with silk around the neck . . . '.

One of the most important ceremonies enacted in both urban and rural Muslim Tunisian weddings is the *jilwa*, which requires the bride to present herself to her own relatives, then to the relatives of the groom, veiled and unveiled. Throughout the ceremony she performs a series of ritualised gestures. In Sfax, the bride, dressed in seven different tunics, stands on a platform and executes specific movements with her eyes closed (Zouari 1980:158). She is displayed to the assembled guests and unveiled. She retires to a separate room, removes the top tunic and returns to repeat the performance. This continues until she is wearing the seventh tunic, the richest of all. She sits on a chair, her face again covered, her hands resting on her breasts. In the evening of the same day, a similar routine takes place, this time in her future husband's home. The *jilwa* provides the means to present the bride to her husband and others in a formal setting, in an advantageous array of splendid costumes prepared with time and care. Thus, the bride's essential attributes of beauty and modesty are once again perfectly captured.

Fertility and Protection

Many of the costume decisions regarding material, designs and colours are closely linked to concerns about fertility, as the prime objective in marriages throughout North Africa is to produce children, thus continuing the family line. The sometimes complicated subterfuges enacted in an attempt to avert misfortune and secure this ideal can readily be seen through the use of clothing. The adoption of textile items used for the first time at the marriage ceremonies marks the beginning of the transition from childhood to adulthood.

The Fes (Morocco) bride is completely surrounded by piles of richly-covered cushions and mattresses. She is draped in layers of fine materials and voluminous 'sleeves' are pinned to the back wall. Thus she is transformed into a splendid, though barely visible, display. From J. Jouin, 'Iconographie de la mariée citadine dans l'Islam nord-africain', *Revue des Études Islamiques*, 1931, 5:327.

The bride is transported to the groom's house on the back of a horse, with a young boy sitting on the saddle in front of her. She is dressed in clothing provided for the wedding by the groom and her face is concealed. The small male child is thought to bring her good luck. *Photo: Royal Anthropological Institute.*

The occurrence of knots and belts in wedding ceremonies is of particular importance as they relate to virginity, fertility and unity. In Omdurman (Sudan) the bride was wrapped in strips of material tightly knotted together round her waist and hips over her clothes. The groom was obliged to untie the knots on the evening of the seventh day after the marriage ceremony, the bride all the while attempting to stop him. The meaning here is twofold: the knots served as a physical as well as symbolic obstacle to the consummation of the marriage. The bride in her attempts to resist these advances was protecting her virginity and thus preserving her honour.

In Sudan, in the suburban village of Buurri al Lamaab, outside Khartoum, a further instance of tying is noted during the *jirtiq* ceremony, at which the bride and groom are ritually invested with ornaments proper to their new status. The essential *jirtiq* item consists of strands of red silk threaded with a blue or green

73

RIGHT Embroidered cotton trousers from Siwa Oasis, Egypt. Girls may prepare seven pairs of trousers in anticipation of marriage. These will be worn during the wedding celebrations, and will continue in use afterwards as everyday under-garments. The colours and motifs employed, knowledge of which is apparently passed from mother to daughter, are also seen on both their black and white ceremonial dresses. L:89 cm; w:74 cm. 1991,Af11.2.

LEFT In the Tunisian village of Raf-Raf, tunics such as this would be worn on the third day of the wedding celebrations by the bride as an outer-garment. They are known as tattooed (*mwashma*), due to the resemblance between the embroidered motifs and certain designs painted onto women's hands. Flower patterns are embroidered in brightly coloured wool onto the base material and the net sleeves, and are enlivened by the use of sequins. Popular good-luck symbols, such as the fish, crescent, star, birds and a form of the 'tree of life' occur throughout. L:110 cm; w:116 cm. 1991,Af15.1.

bead, often terminating in a silk tassel. Both the bride and groom wear one of these on their right wrist or forearm. They will not be removed until at least seven days after completion of the wedding ceremonies. It is interesting to note that red silk threads occur in other marriage celebrations in North Africa. On the henna night in Tripoli (Abdelkafi 1977:60), the bride has one silk thread passed over her left knee and a second across her mouth, tied at her neck, with a sugar lump placed under her tongue. After the ceremonies these threads are severed and the pieces tossed over the heads of gathered female friends, in the hope that they, too, will soon find marriage partners. The thread in her mouth indicates that the bride will not be loquacious and her speech will always be sweet. The silk thread around her knee expresses the hope that she will be attached to her home (camels were hobbled at the knee to prevent them wandering from the tent). In these cases, it would seem that not only the materials and colours, but also the acts of tying and then breaking or removing the threads are of importance. The acceptance of a new union through marriage is demonstrated by the tying of the red silk threads, balanced by recognition of the separation from childhood, as witnessed through severance of the same threads and in the act of scattering them over the heads of the bride's friends.

On the evening of the *jirtiq*, a variation on the *hizama* ceremony (the undoing of the belt) is performed. The bride is dressed in her husband's trousers which, however, she wears back to front. The trousers are fastened by means of lacings which are wetted and tied tightly, rendering them difficult to undo. The lacings now face the front, so the act of forcibly untying them is explicitly sexual. As in the northern Sudanese ceremony, the bride is expected to resist these attempts. Moroccan brides also have been observed to have seven knots tied in their trousers through which the groom is obliged to pick his way before consummating the marriage. Once successfully completed, the groom can be seen to have symbolically achieved his goal, that of gaining entry; the bride also has completed her duty: defence of her honour and subsequent submission.

It is customary throughout North Africa for the bride to remove her belt between *lailat al-hinna'* and *lailat al-dukhla*. It has been suggested that any form of constriction during this time would hinder the process of conception. At the end of this tense and potent period, a belt is once more tied around the bride's waist at a special ceremony called *tahzim* (putting on the belt). This event also indicates that the bride is felt to be in less danger from disruptive forces, highlighting the beginning of her new life and demonstrating that she is now ready to resume a normal existence. This action is rarely performed by the woman herself but will be undertaken by selected individuals. It may be re-tied by her mother-in-law, indicating acceptance and entry into a new family and a new role, by a woman with male children, or by small boys, in the hope that she will have sons. In Andjra (Morocco) the bride's belt was tied by an uncircumcised boy.

During the period between the wedding day and the seventh day the bride, especially, may be variously viewed as dangerous, in danger or polluted. In order to combat this precarious state she often appears draped in a veil or shawl. Brides in Omdurman are covered head to foot in a multicoloured silk shawl (*qarmasis*), which is designed to protect them from bad luck at this stage. The shawl, originating in India, was one of the goods traded into the area from the Red Sea ports. It is used at marriage, on the occasion of the birth of a child and to cover a newly-circumcised girl or boy. These are all events associated with blood and thus pollution. People at these periods are felt to be in danger from malevolent forces, hence the shiny effect of the shawl may be seen to repel or attract.

A recurring means of countering misfortune is for men to adopt items of female dress and for women to wear male costume. During the *jirtiq* ceremony in northern Sudan, the groom wears a fine silk *thawb* such as women use. When venturing outside between *yawm al-dukhla* and the seventh day, he will cover his head and face in a woman's veil.

It is noteworthy that in several groups throughout North Africa, the bride, when appearing in public during the marriage festivities, is covered from head to foot in her future husband's white wool cloak (*jird*). She wears this covering from leaving her own home until consummation of the marriage; after this transitory period she re-appears wearing married women's clothes for the first time. Thus she moves from childhood, secure in her father's house to a new home and status. By adopting the *jird* she is concealed from malicious influences, symbolically protected by her future husband for the first time.

Further protection against the dangers of the evil eye is sought by dressing friends of the bride or groom in an identical fashion. In Morocco, when the bride travels from her own home to the groom's house, she will be accompanied by female friends and relatives, a few of whom may be dressed similarly in an attempt to distract the harmful influence of the evil eye. In Egypt, on the *lailat al-dukhla*, the groom was accompanied by two friends who were dressed as he was in a red striped caftan, red *jubba* and a red silk turban.

Bride and groom are united legally through the marriage contract, but symbolically in numerous other ways. Certain times of the day are deemed especially potent and the newly-married pair have recourse to various evasive actions. In the northern Sudan, at sunrise and sunset – dangerous periods when it is believed the spirits are active – the couple participate in the *hadana* ceremony. They sit or lie together quietly with the bride's coloured silk veil placed over their heads. Not only does this serve as protection against malevolent spirits, it emphasises their unique state which signifies their new union.

Dress and New Status

The bride and groom may adopt new items of dress during, or immediately following, the marriage ceremonies. These may indicate their special status, or be used as a comment on personal beliefs and values. Perhaps most importantly, clothing may ease their transition from unmarried to married state, and their own and others' acceptance of this state. In Nubia, the Kenuz bride wears a white floor-length cloak (*shuqqa*) which she continues to use for the rest of her life. It is seen as a visible indication of marriage, declaring that the bride is now deemed socially and religiously 'mature'. Upon marriage in Omdurman, the bride dresses in the *qurbab* which is simply a long piece of material wrapped twice around her waist; the wealth and status of her husband will be reflected in the type of material chosen. The brides of Ghadames Oasis (Libya) are assisted by girls of their age-group in dressing in the married woman's costume for the first time; this is always red, either a woollen gown or a 'Sudanese' cotton gown. The following day the bride dresses herself, but puts on her white decorated dress upside down, pretending she doesn't know how to wear this unfamiliar item of clothing, thus indicating her novice-status as a married woman. The use of red woollen belts among the Bedouin women of Egypt's Western Desert has been discussed in detail by Abu-Lughod (1986:134): 'The red belt that every married woman wears symbolizes her fertility and association with the creation of life'. It serves not only as a symbol of a woman's marital status but as a declaration of her positive reproductive powers. It is an essential article of clothing – women may be viewed as 'shameful' if they discard it.

Changes in the type of headwear adopted are a common means of indicating visibly the transition from young, unmarried girl to married woman. The bride's hair is revealed during many marriage ceremonies in North Africa and elaborately dressed in a style appropriate to her new status. She then assumes head-dresses or caps worn exclusively by married women, which will completely cover the hair; these will often be worn for the rest of her life, especially when outside the immediate home environment. Annually, during September, on the Imilchil plateau in the High Atlas mountains (Morocco), members of the Ayt Hadiddu tribe converge to combine market trading, the celebration of a saint's day and the search for a marriage partner. The Berber women are all dressed alike in simple white robes, with their striped woollen cloaks wrapped around their shoulders. They don head-dresses around which they wind brightly coloured head-ropes, sparkling with sequins. In this case, widowed or divorced women are easily identified by the exaggerated point on their stiff head-dresses, while virgins wear similarly decorated, flat, rounded hoods.

Libyan girls from Ghadames Oasis adopt the married woman's red woollen

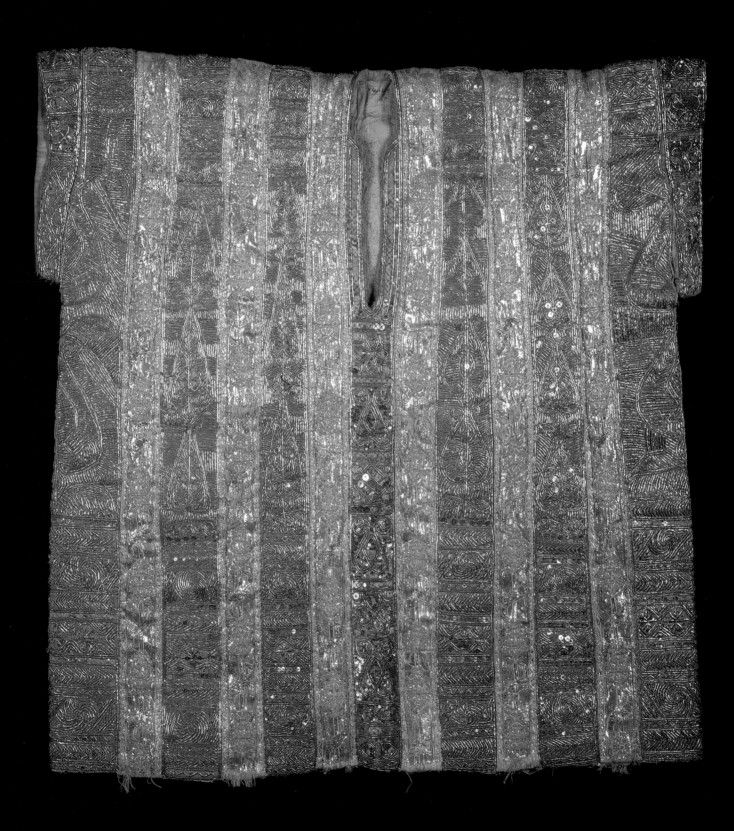

LEFT The Tunisian wedding tunic has gradually acquired a greater degree of elaboration through the introduction of sumptuous materials and an increasing emphasis on gold-work as the primary decorative element. The formerly supple tunic has been rendered almost rigid by the use of cardboard backing, which is decorated with flat gold thread (*tal*), in geometric, floral and amuletic-inspired designs. The base material has been entirely subsumed by the mass of sequins and gold-work currently in fashion. In this vast costume the bride is rendered virtually immobile and is almost completely concealed.
L:111 cm; W:106 cm. 1991,Af4.1.

RIGHT, ABOVE Detail from a woman's dress from Bahriya Oasis, Egypt. The embroidery is in purple, yellow and white cotton thread on a heavy black cotton base. Special attention is paid to the decoration on the back hems of dresses, as this area would show below the shawl or head-covering. These labour-intensive clothes were produced by young girls, under the supervision of female relatives, in preparation for marriage. Today they are worn only by older women or on special occasions.
L:125 cm; W:129 cm. 1991,Af11.5.

RIGHT, BELOW Woollen cloths from Ghadames Oasis, Libya, used on the henna night immediately before the wedding festivities. Whereas the bride will have hands and feet dyed, only the right hand of the groom is rubbed with henna. The use of henna is viewed as both purifying and protective: it is thought to be imbued with *baraka* (blessing). The colour red which recurs throughout the marriage ceremonies is clearly associated with blood and thus fertility. Once the henna has been applied, bags or wrapping cloths may be used to prevent the dye rubbing off or staining clothing. L:57 cm; W:43 cm. 1981,Af5.4–7.

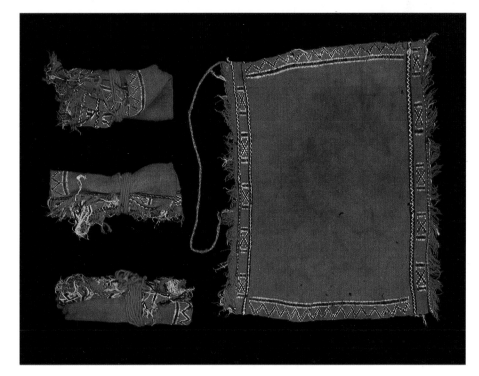

head-cloth (*almarfad*) prior to the ritual bath. This loosely woven rectangular shawl is fringed at both ends and decorated with thin black and white stripes. In Morocco the new bride was exhibited on the sixth day after marriage equipped with her new headwear. She would wear a triangular pad (*hantoz*), covered with silk handkerchieves embroidered in gold thread.

There are restrictions placed on the use of clothing and types of dress adopted in the days immediately following the marriage celebrations. It is generally believed that the bride and groom are still in a polluted state; they often remain separated from members of the family and friends or may even enter into complete seclusion for a limited period. In certain parts of North Africa the wedding clothes will continue to be worn for up to 40 days after marriage, before being discarded, whereupon clothes associated with their newly married state can be adopted.

The Kenuz bridegroom would continue to wear his marriage costume for seven days, due to fears about the evil eye which was thought to induce impotence. After this period, it would be safe to discard his costume and assume fully his new status. Only after a period of isolation lasting forty days would the Sudanese bride and groom wear everyday clothes. Until then they continued to use their wedding costumes, which they were forbidden to wash. Once their period of separation was completed, they could cleanse themselves; thus purified, they were able to start their new lives.

Within other groups it is acceptable to wear parts of the wedding costume on future occasions. The significance and symbolism of textiles used in marriage fluctuates as the context in which they are worn alters or when the role of the individual is modified. Jewish women in Morocco regularly wore their gold-embroidered velvet wedding outfits when attending circumcisions, other weddings, or community celebrations. The women of Siwa Oasis (Egypt) make and embroider seven pairs of trousers for use during the marriage ceremonies; afterwards these will be worn as everyday articles of clothing. Removed from their primary context, textiles may lose their special significance; new functions are added and different messages conveyed.

Although visually the marriage costumes of women from urban and rural communities may appear to differ considerably – the former being markedly more opulent with an abundance of gold thread, braid and sequins – there is a unifying determinant for the choice of clothing. In rural areas, brides are covered with their future husband's cloaks or with bulky woollen veils, often becoming rather shapeless bundles. They are thus rendered safe from envious glances or acts of malice; conversely, family members and friends are protected from their polluting influences. Similarly, if one looks beyond the 'glint of gold', the shape of the urban Tunisian tunics and the Moroccan robes is admirably designed to disguise or conceal the female form. However, the motivation for adopting such a concealing costume may now lie in a desire to display publicly family wealth, through the excessive use of luxurious materials which create an impression of opulence.

Innovations such as the Western-style white wedding dress may be viewed as fashion statements adopted by the urban elite and often copied by migrant workers on their return to rural districts. Weyland (1993:162), writing about an Egyptian village in the Delta comments: 'today marriage has become one of the obvious vehicles for the introduction of urban life-styles into rural society'. Villagers in this area are 'borrowing' the white European wedding dress and

An Egyptian bride wearing an elaborate white European-style wedding dress and veil. The choice of this costume serves to proclaim the wealth of the family and establishes the bride as a 'modern' woman. *Photo: J. Mellors*.

with it new notions of sophistication, cleanliness and purity. White is viewed as *nazafa*, clean and pure, far removed from the harsh realities of life. The mud-brick houses, earth floors and all-pervading dust, along with the traditional agricultural occupations, constitute an inexorable battle with dirt. The use of the European wedding dress marks a new development and acts as a means of introducing urban styles into village life.

5

TEXTILES OF TOWN AND COUNTRY

Patterned cotton dress from Algeria. Women and young girls wear vivid, printed cotton or synthetic dresses around the home, their heads wrapped in bright scarves. The dresses are made up by village dressmakers or by the women themselves, so that innovations in style will be introduced only gradually. L:120 cm; w:119 cm. 1974,Af20.66.

An attempt to distinguish between urban and rural textiles in North Africa may be a means of highlighting historical and cultural factors. However, it may also impose an inaccurate and artificial barrier between these areas. Such distinctions as there are may be viewed as the outcome of differences in physical and social environment, education and occupation, as well as a response to economic conditions. The evolution of dress styles and the accelerated impact of external clothing innovations in urban North Africa reflect the society's struggle for identity and stability in the face of growing industrialisation.

One of the most powerful and far-reaching influences on female dress styles and attitudes to clothing has arisen through increased access to education for women and girls. Admission into educational establishments beyond primary level has enabled certain female students in North Africa to compete against, and study with, their male contemporaries. The career opportunities facilitated by education, and the ability to meet and integrate socially with members of the opposite sex, in a defined environment, has raised interesting – and, at times, challenging – questions about the ever-present concern with women's 'modesty'.

Concerns about mixed-gender classes and female dress are first witnessed at puberty; prior to this stage boys and girls in North African society mix freely. Young boys frequently accompany their mothers in the daily routine, helping with minor domestic tasks beside their sisters. There is little obvious differentiation between male and female dress. At this period lower-class children especially may be regarded as 'sexless' (Rugh 1986:131). The implication is that they have not attained an age at which the 'dangers' of their different genders are fully exposed. Young girls and boys attend the same school classes. However, with the onset of puberty, female attendance may drop. Female education beyond primary level continues to be regarded as being of lesser importance compared with the higher educational levels which boys may be encouraged to achieve. Girls who are allowed, or encouraged, to attend further school classes face increased concern about their personal appearance and their adherence to publicly accepted notions of modesty.

These concerns may be alleviated by an increased use of 'modesty garments', which signal a public, rather than personal, commitment to upholding appropriate standards of moral behaviour. In northern Sudan the *thawb* (female garment) was adopted by pubescent girls continuing in education; formerly, this article was reserved for married women. Thus, the ambiguous position of young women involved in mixed-gender education may be reflected in their earlier use of modest clothing. The message conveyed establishes their honourable intentions, while reflecting the ambiguities of their situation. It

Bedouin women preparing food outside a tent, south of the town of Batna, Algeria. Both of the women wear floral print dresses of a Western-inspired design. *Photo: M. W. Hilton-Simpson, courtesy of the Royal Anthropological Institute.*

emphasises the difficulties North African societies encounter in attempting to accommodate female vocational, technical or higher educational opportunities.

When female students are placed in a seemingly hostile and alien educational institution, formerly viewed as an exclusively male domain, the use of modesty garments creates a feeling of security and reinforces ideas about a common identity. In pursuing further education, which might increase their personal and social prospects, they expose themselves to taunts of immodesty. They may endure the contradiction of liberty within the confines of a co-educational establishment, with restricted activity on return to family life. In learning to balance these two life-styles, women face increasing, and sometimes overwhelming, pressures.

The use of 'Islamic dress' (*ziyy islami*) became noticeable among female university students in Cairo during the 1970's. At this time, the emphasis was on sombre, loose, full-length outfits with close-fitting headwear (*higab*). However, by the early 1980's a modified version of this garment had gained popularity, becoming a fashionable outfit among lower-middle class working

Beni Ourain shawl (*handira*) from Morocco. The subtle use of colour and the numerous complex design bands are characteristic of shawls from this area. The luxurious pile, which is produced by leaving the ivory-coloured wool wefts loose, provides both a decorative effect and additional warmth. L:158 cm; w:100 cm. 1994,Af12.1.

women. The *muhaggaba* (those who are veiled) favoured form-fitting colourful garments, frequently made of silky materials; their heads were covered with attractive gauzy scarves. The initial impetus for adopting the outfit appears to have evolved to suit the tastes of the majority, who for reasons of class, conflict, peer pressure or a need to reconcile their 'traditional' and 'modern' roles have chosen to wear it. The complex and diverse reasons expressed for this choice demonstrate women's personal internal struggles and their attempts to present an acceptable 'public face'. The costume may signify a heightened interest in, or reliance on, formal religion, or it may be a means of avoiding unsolicited male attention in the working environment, or on the notoriously over-crowded public transport system. It also serves as an effective means of communicating middle-class aspirations and expectations in an acceptable, honourable and unpresumptuous way. By dressing in a recognised middle-class manner, women are able to reinforce or assert their social mobility. Some women have political reasons for choosing this dress style, employing it as a subtle means of pronouncing their rejection of government economic and social policies. The use of fully-concealing clothes may be viewed in different

A hooded woollen jacket (*jallaba*) used by a young boy of the Chleuh Berbers, Morocco, while helping to herd and move sheep. It is woven in fairly coarse wool edged with distinctive red and white braid in a chevron design, which may be a protective device. The geometric motifs are woven in slit-tapestry technique in red, white, yellow, orange, blue and green wool. They decorate the hood, chest and upper back of the garment. L:88 cm; w:84 cm. 1987,Af11.1.

A woollen shawl (*handira*), worn by women of the Ayt Morrhad group, based in the High Atlas mountains, Morocco. The broad red and black bands are relieved by thin counter-twined stripes, produced by twisting a single white thread with two black threads. Tribal affiliation may be demonstrated by the specific combination of colours and bands. L:176 cm; w:120 cm. 1969,Af32.2.

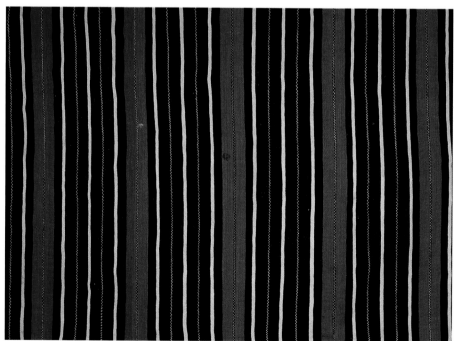

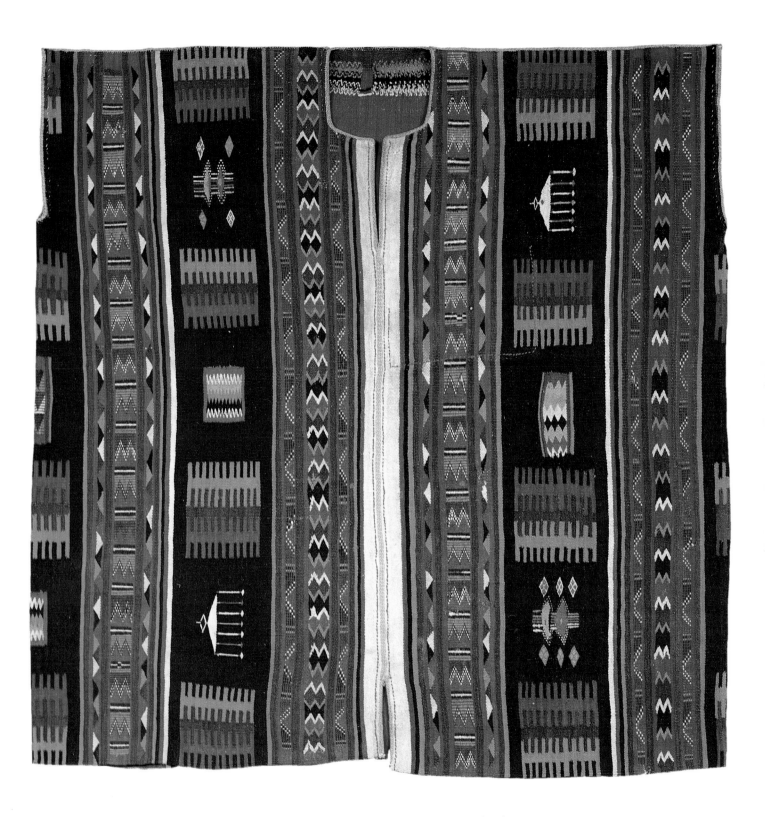

Tapestry-woven woollen tunic (*gandura*) from the Mzab, Algeria.
Woven by women for their sons, these striking tunics are worn in
winter months. The named design elements include birds with their
young, pomegranate seeds, couscous grains, keys, forks and a
table with guests, emphasising the harmony and domesticity
of life within the community. L:92 cm; w:78 cm. 1910,5–3.2.

Professional people frequently assume Western-inspired clothing in North Africa; a popular option among men in Egypt is a variation on the European 'safari' suit of the colonial period. In summer months, a short-sleeved version is available. *Photo: A. Dodson.*

ways but, in general, it proclaims the woman as one who observes the outward symbols of modest behaviour.

Economic exigences as well as increased educational opportunities have drawn women into full-time employment outside the home. A complex mix of social factors determines whether this decision will enhance or reduce their status. The use of uniforms and modesty outfits may ease the transition, establishing acceptable 'social distance', while adoption of foreign styles may present a new image, facilitating social mobility.

Young women who work in large hotels as waitresses or receptionists are constantly exposed to contact with predominantly male 'strangers'. The inherent nature of this type of work necessitates a certain level of polite social interaction, whether in the form of helpful discourse or by serving food and drink. Exposure to such potentially awkward and culturally difficult situations on a daily basis obliges women to avoid any provocative behaviour. The provision of uniforms helps to protect and socially distance them from unknown strangers.

In the Sudan, women were employed as air hostesses for the first time in 1964. The prevalent image of attractive, well-groomed young women tending to the needs of an unrelated male clientele conflicted with deep concerns about modesty. Further anxiety surrounded the disposal of the *thawb* and the necessity of travelling to foreign countries alone (i.e. without family members) on a regular basis. Once again, uniforms helped to ease this transition; they did not replace modesty garments, or in any way substitute for the *thawb*, but acted as a means of relaying a message of distance and authority that ordinary modern or western-derived clothing could not.

Uniforms may also be worn for practical reasons when machinery, technical equipment or physical activity is involved. Today, nurses and midwives in the Sudan wear uniforms based on those used by British nurses, which were introduced into the country at the beginning of this century, following the establishment of condominion rule. Their heads are covered by a white *tarha* (head veil), which affords them physical freedom, while simultaneously safeguarding their reputation as respectable women. Men, also, are obliged to discard their traditional modes of dress in certain working situations. The male

RIGHT Habbaniya (Baqqara) women from southern Darfur swathed in the colourful printed *thawb*. It was formerly exclusively a married woman's garment. However, with increased access to education, young girls began to wear the *thawb* to school and college. The garment has been celebrated in songs, and new styles are named after significant social and political events. *Photo: P. Wilson.*

villagers of Kafr el-Elow (Egypt) who are employed in local factories are required by law to wear a shirt and khaki trousers, popularly known as 'national dress' (*al-badla al-sha'biya*). The traditional loose, flowing men's gown (*gallabiya*) might prove hazardous when working with machinery (Fakhouri 1972:20).

Agricultural workers wear clothing suited to this activity; thus women may be obliged to discard garments normally associated with perceptions of modesty when involved in physical labour. Although dress may be modified in such exceptional circumstances, the women involved may suffer a loss of status in the community. This phenomenon is particularly clearly represented in the Tunisian village of Sidi Ameur, where two social factions co-reside. The claim of one group (the Zawiya) to higher social status and politico-economic privileges is asserted by the men through the continued seclusion of their women. They remain inside their homes and, on leaving, wear the *safsari*, a large white rectangular cloth which covers all but the upper face, hands and feet. Recently, these women have reasserted their superiority by adopting Western-style dresses while at home, in preference to the traditional blouse and wrap-skirt (Abu Zahra 1982:156). In comparison, the second group of women (the Ramada), are obliged to work in the fields, where not only do they mix freely with men, but also continue to wear the traditional rural dress, the *takhlila*, which exposes their arms and faces. The *takhlila* is a large rectangular cloth, variously coloured according to locality. The Ramada women favour red. It is wrapped around the body, fastened at the waist by a belt, thus leaving the arms free to undertake physical activity (Abu Zahra 1982:168). The Ramada women are thus seen to transgress the modesty code in numerous ways: through dress and interaction with male workers, they are exposing themselves and their families to ridicule and re-inforcing their inferior social standing in the community. They are also seen as personally 'shameless': by appearing thus attired in a public place, their behaviour is judged as inappropriate. In addition, they are not able to follow innovative styles and modes of dress, which may be seen as social enhancers; thus their use of costume relays negative messages.

Environment and Economy

The effects of environment and the markers of economic stability are clearly reflected in the choice of clothing materials, forms and designs in North Africa. In many rural areas, where the concept of tribal affiliation or kinship group still applies, costume decisions may be made according to well-established and locally-accepted customs. In addition, owing to their isolated positions, innovative foreign styles may take longer to infiltrate, so that new materials, styles or decorative elements will emerge only gradually. In the racially, ethnically and socially diverse towns, which support both the influx of people from abroad and rural migrants, a more diverse range of clothing may be more widely accessible.

In rural areas of the Maghrib, the predominantly Berber-speaking populations rely on access to raw materials which are essential in what remains a low-cash economy. Historically, due to regular transhumance, textiles needed to fulfil multiple functions. Women frequently supply the skills and labour to produce the requisite clothing and textile items for their families. These articles are invariably woven in wool or in combination with goat's hair in fairly

Moroccan women from the Rheris river region wearing draped dresses secured at the shoulders with fibulae and fastened around the waist with belts. The versatility of their stout cloaks is demonstrated by their use in this instance as carriers.
Photo: M. Morin-Barde.

A hooded cloak (*akhnif*) made of wool and goat's hair from the Ouaouzguit region, Morocco. These cloaks were ingeniously woven in a semi-circular shape on vertical looms. The distinctive orange-red 'eye' design was elaborated with supplementary weft patterning, with embroidered geometric motifs added by men. Adult Jews were permitted to wear these cloaks with the constraint that the design faced inwards. L:124 cm; w:355 cm. +5773.

uniform styles and sizes, in accordance with their tribal allegiances. They may produce textiles solely for use by the tribal group, or create an excess, which may then be taken to sell at the weekly *suq*.

The ubiquitous rectangular tunics, hooded cloaks and loose wrapping cloths seen throughout the Maghrib since Pre-Islamic times, have survived in some rural areas today. Men from differing religious, social or tribal groups wore a wool or cotton tunic and trousers, covered by a simple, draped cloak and, in the winter, a densely woven woollen robe with a hood. These items were admirably suited to the sometimes harsh environmental conditions endured by the rural population, being hard-wearing, warm and interchangeable as clothing or bedding. Increasingly, woollen garments have been replaced by imported cotton and, occasionally, silk. Although the cloaks and tunics assumed specific names, and varied in length and decoration throughout the countries of the Maghrib, these items of male clothing have shown remarkable persistence and homogeneity.

In contrast, women's costumes, although showing a certain level of consistency, vary enormously in colour, design combinations and, most especially, in the use of head-coverings. The messages conveyed by the adoption or rejection of certain articles may reveal origin or tribal allegiances, status changes, as well as individual aesthetic choices. Rural women throughout the Maghrib are distinguished by their use of draped, rather than tailored, clothing. This form of covering was also known in Egypt; Lane (1871 vol. 1:62),

90

Ayt Brahim woman from the High Atlas, Morocco, carrying her baby in her cloak. Narrow white stripes separate the broader blue, black and occasional red bands.
Photo: M. Morin-Barde.

describing the dress of lower-class women, wrote: 'most of the women envelop themselves in a large piece of dark-brown woollen stuff . . . wrapping it round the body, and attaching the upper parts together over each shoulder . . . '. He includes a plate which shows a form of the dress similar to those still used in rural areas of the Maghrib. The antiquity of the style cannot be doubted, nor its widespread appeal.

In the Maghrib, this basic 'dress' is composed of a large rectangular cloth skilfully wrapped around the body and secured by fibulae. Belts of wool, or synthetic materials of brilliant colours are worn, wound several times around the waist. Unlike the sombre colours of men's cloaks, women's shawls are often finely woven with delicate, intricate designs, bold bands of colour or subtle combinations of perfectly balanced geometric designs. These loose, sturdy shawls and cloaks assume many different guises, being used as modesty garments, bedding, baby carriers or sacks for the transport of food, fuel or market goods.

Choices made about clothing traditionally may have been based on geographical location and environment as much as cultural and economic factors, as seen among the various groups inhabiting Egypt's marginal rural areas. The Bedouin of the Eastern Desert and Sinai, the oasis dwellers and the inhabitants of some Upper Egyptian villages, due to their isolated locations and self-sufficient life-styles, relied on easily accessible, sturdy materials to form the basis of their garments. Female clothes were lavishly embroidered in colourful

Young women from an oasis in Egypt's Western Desert, wearing cotton print dresses with 'foreign' elements such as cuffs, collars, a breast pocket, decorative piping and a buttoned placket front opening. Unmarried girls frequently wear long, loose trousers in line with locally accepted notions of modesty.
Photo: C. Spring.

silks, which alleviated the sombre black base material; designs and dress styles followed specific patterns which allowed identification on both geographical and cultural grounds. Today, with improved communication networks and increased rural migrancy, the village and oasis dwellers in particular have greater access to urban goods and styles. Younger women are discarding their traditional garments in favour of urban-influenced styles, wearing floral print dresses in forms popular throughout the country. A woman in the oasis of Bahriya comments on her knowledge of fashionable styles: 'When I go to Cairo on the bus, I wear a dress that is fitted at the waist and sometimes on visits to people there I wear short foreign-style dresses. People here in Bawiti [major town in oasis] know how to dress!' (Rugh 1986:112).

However, married women in Siwa Oasis continue to wear the *derfudit*, a blue and white checked cloth, which has been imported from the village of Kerdassa near Giza for decades. This is always worn when outside the house and covers from the head to below the waist. Almost the only view of women gained by the casual visitor to Siwa will be fleeting glimpses of figures swathed in these distinctive cloths.

Cut-and-sewn clothes, seen predominantly in the towns, are more costly owing to the wastage of material and increased labour time. They may also be embellished with expensive materials such as braids, ribbons and sequins, or be embroidered in silks, or gold and silver threads. Thus, not only are town dwellers influenced by the range of materials before them, but their choice relies on their ability to pay for these additional luxuries. This, in turn, reflects the pressures placed on the urban middle and upper classes to establish prestige and status through visual display.

Lower-class urban populations, due to economic restrictions, continue to rely on locally-produced or government-subsidised materials. They are also constrained by cultural considerations relating to notions of modesty, and are bound by locally imposed 'standards' of dress. However, innovations are assimilated gradually and 'modern' details such as pockets, collars, cuffs, zips and buttons appear on both male and female costumes. These additions, which increase the cost of a garment, serve to delineate the 'sophisticated' urban lower-classes from the 'unsophisticated' rural poor.

External Influences

Repeated foreign invasions, occupations and migrations have inevitably left their mark on North African society. Traces of these activities are seen in dress styles, borrowed terms, imported materials and design influences, as well as in the preserved dress traditions of non-indigenous people. Adoption of garments which have external influences may communicate wealth, status or prestige within the community, or, negatively, may arouse suspicion, alienation or avoidance.

While the countries of North Africa have been variously influenced by Turkish, Andalusian and European styles, their Jewish populations have endeavoured to preserve their unique cultural identity through the continued use of traditional costumes and their undoubted artistic skills as specialists in metal thread embroidery and tablet weaving. Although external influences may filter down the economic scale, foreign elements are essentially an urban phenomenon, fully embraced by the wealthy citizens, while only partially adopted by the urban lower classes.

Group of boys from an oasis in the Western Desert of Egypt. It is common to see some young boys wearing brightly coloured synthetic tracksuits and tee-shirts, alongside others in the simple cotton *gallabiya*. Men and boys travel more frequently than women, thus experiencing a wider range of costume styles and materials. *Photo: J. Hudson.*

A street in Algiers during the 1920s showing women heavily veiled, holding their cloaks around them. The extravagantly billowing trousers (*shintiyan*) are derived from Turkish forms. *Photo: Courtesy of the Royal Geographical Society, London.*

The Arab invaders of Egypt and North Africa borrowed little in the way of costume from the indigenous people of the region. Thus, at this early stage, a visible division between the rural communities and the conquering Arabs, who resided in urban centres, was established. During the fifteenth century, Andalusian fashions spread to Morocco via Moorish and Jewish immigrants. The majority of these people settled in the urban centres, thus further stimulating the diversity of costume choices open to their inhabitants.

Certain items of foreign dress were especially favoured. The Turkish *qaftan*, a long robe with sleeves, was used by both men and women throughout North Africa, utilising rich silks and lavishly decorated with floral motifs in silk and metal threads. In the Maghrib, bi-coloured tunics became popular. It is thought that they were introduced into the area by Andalusians (Sethom 1969:10–11). Tunics such as these are still worn for ceremonial or festive occasions, especially in Tunisia. The 'aba', a short, sleeveless, outer coat, was worn in Egypt, mainly by men. It was produced in various materials to reflect the status and wealth of the wearer. The widespread use of this garment throughout the Middle East, where it was worn by both men and women, has been ably documented; it is from this area that the Egyptian version was undoubtedly copied (Dozy 1845:292–297).

Waistcoats remain popular in North Africa: in Egypt the *sidar*, which Lane described as 'a short vest of cloth, or of striped coloured silk and cotton, without sleeves' (1871 vol.1:36) is still worn. In Libya and Tunisia, short waistcoats known as *farmala* are worn. These were probably derived from Turkish forms, which were introduced into Tunisia in the eighteenth century. A further development – the characteristic stiff gold 'wings' which embellish some Tunisian waistcoats – possibly developed as a result of Andalusian influence. In this form, the elaborate decoration could be seen under the sleeveless outer tunics.

In the towns of North Africa, where tunics and robes were frequently used, trousers became an essential item of clothing for fashionable ladies. Revault

ABOVE During the nineteenth and early twentieth centuries, wealthy women in urban Tunisia would cover their heads and faces with an 'ajar on leaving their homes. Traditionally, in elite households throughout North Africa, seclusion was equated with wealth and economic stability. The use of the luxurious silk 'ajar demonstrated visibly both honourable intent and family wealth. From L. Bertholon and E. Chantre, *Berbérie Orientale*, Lyons, 1913, vol. 1:460.

LEFT Veils such as this were initially produced in Tunisia in the village of Testour by families of Andalusian origin. The veils ('ajar) have central transparent black rectangles, which allow women to see, without exposing their faces to strangers. The elaborately decorated end panels draw on motifs influenced by Turkey and Andalusia. By means of careful draping the intricacy of this decoration was artfully displayed. L:150 cm; w:102 cm. 1995,Af4.1.

RIGHT Women from the Egyptian village of Naqada produce these textiles using the treadle loom – operated in other parts of Africa exclusively by men – and employ silk or, increasingly, synthetic fibres to produce modesty garments (*milaya*). These used to be exported to Libya and Sudan for use by women as wraps or shawls. L:142 cm; w:58 cm. 1994,Af24.4.

(1960: n. 10) commented: 'the end of last century is marked by the appearance of a Turkish female costume, characterised by . . . wide and baggy trousers'. The fashion was initially adopted by the elite, but rapidly became popular among all classes. The trousers (*shintiyan*) were extraordinarily wide; their distinctive billowing shape was achieved by the use of drawstrings at the ends, which were tied up under the knee, thus releasing a mass of material to the ankles. Gradually, and again following the lead of Turkey, trousers which narrowed from knee to ankle became the trend. The finest of these were heavily embroidered in silk, or gold thread, so that the decoration showed below the tunic.

The Andalusian ceremonial costume, the *kiswat al-kabira*, worn by immigrant Jewish women in Morocco, is one of the most striking examples of an imported form. Its uniqueness lies in the fact that the entire costume, instead of individual elements, has been retained. The ensemble is well-known in other countries with established Jewish communities. The Spanish derivation of its form has been widely acknowledged. The costume is composed of three main elements: a wrap-around skirt (*zaltita*), a short-sleeved jacket (*kumbayz*), and a plastron (*katif*). The individual names of these pieces differ according to region, as does the opulent gold work decorating the costume.

In the late nineteenth and early twentieth centuries, increasing European influence in the North African economy, its politics and culture, led to a marked change in costume styles, especially by the urban elite. The luxurious, flowing, garments copied from Turkey and the elaborately embroidered Andalusian-inspired styles were gradually replaced by seemingly rather uncomfortable, form-fitting clothes which imitated European clothing. North African men who regularly travelled abroad or had business contacts with Europeans adopted suits, shirts and ties. These clothes, which reflected a growing economic dependence on Europe, conferred notions of prestige and status on the wearers in their working environment. The suit has retained its popularity and is regarded today as standard office wear in the cities and towns of North Africa, its widespread use now weakening claims of elite status. While younger men and boys may persist in wearing western-derived clothing styles at home, some older men revert to their traditional *gallabiya* and *taqiya* outside office hours. One Cairo-born working man expressed his regret at the change: 'Before I used to dress always in a *gallabiyya*; now I am forced to be dressed in a suit, but from time to time I dress in my *baladi-gallabiyya* [native gown] and when I do so, I feel as if I am in paradise' (El-Messiri 1978:76).

Elite women in urban North Africa also imitated European modes of dress: French and English designs were imported direct and were especially valued, providing a comment both on their family wealth and their own personal flair and taste. Today, the dress styles of lower-class urban women may also be linked to connotations of status. Rugh describes the clothing of women from Bulaq, an overcrowded Cairo quarter, who leave for work 'in their high-heeled "moda" shoes and self-conscious in their tight fitting polyester knit skirts, blouses or dresses. They cling to these discomforts as visible reminders to the world of their achieved or aspiring membership in the middle-class society' (1984:13). Conversely, in districts of dense 'stranger infiltration', such as the tourist areas in Egypt, Tunisia and Morocco, there continues to be a greater use of concealing modesty garments among the lower classes. Not only can this be viewed as an attempt to prevent attracting the attention of male strangers, but

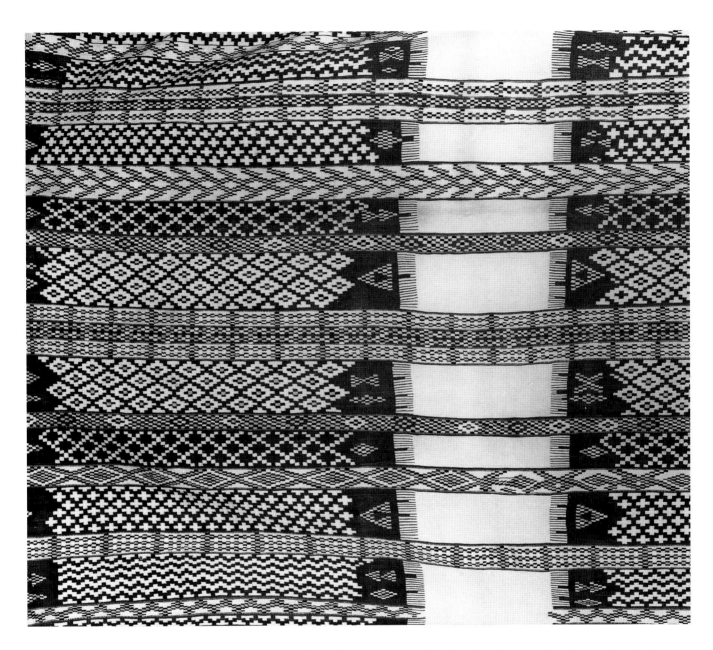

Part of a woman's woollen garment from Algeria, with tapestry-woven blocks of colour. Similarly decorated cloths are known from southern Tunisia. L:156 cm; w:104 cm. 1979,Af1.2673.

also as a public demonstration of their attitude towards safeguarding their own modesty.

Today, the use of imported materials and styles from abroad may be viewed in an ambivalent manner. Men, who have traditionally enjoyed a greater degree of mobility than women, are now exposed to further diversity while working abroad. Foreign textile material is frequently given as a home-coming gift. This may be locally-tailored into the desired 'sophisticated' Middle Eastern styles. In Egypt, a white, semi-transparent, form-fitting *gallabiya* is popular; a style borrowed from the Gulf States. When these are adopted in the village environment, the wearer is easily identified as someone with wider cultural and social experience and in addition, greater disposable wealth. However, these migrants 'no longer conform to the villagers' moral code' (Weyland 1993:202); they may be regarded with suspicion and hostility by older members of the society or those who have not experienced life abroad.

6

BEYOND THE LOOM
NON-WOVEN DESIGNS AND TECHNIQUES

Canvas-backed, appliqué hanging designed in two halves, probably to form the doorway of a large tent. L:285 cm; w:86 cm (left section). L:280 cm; w:85 cm. 1979,Af10.1b&d.

Many of the most spectacular textiles produced in the region are those which have been embellished subsequent to weaving. In all North African countries the craft of embroidery is practised in one form or another, ranging from the sophisticated and intricate work on the costumes of urban Morocco, Tunisia and Ethiopia, to the simpler, but no less striking, embroidered dresses and modesty garments of the Western Desert of Egypt and of Eastern Sudan. Appliqué – the sewing of additional pieces of material to a ready-woven base cloth – is also practised in a number of countries. In Egypt it is employed in the creation of multicoloured, patterned hangings, sometimes of prodigious size, which are used to decorate the interiors of large tents. In Sudan it has long been the means of conveying a religious significance to the distinctive, 'patched' costume of the Sufi initiate, a significance which was dramatically expanded to include a military and political dimension during the existence of the Mahdist state in the late nineteenth century. Other crafts, such as resist-dyeing, plaiting and knitting are to be found in certain areas and represent smaller but still significant contributions to the textile tradition of the region as a whole.

Patches of Humility and Power: the politics of costume and the evolution of the Mahdist *jubba* in nineteenth-century Sudan

The nineteenth century witnessed a period of increasing unrest amongst the peoples of central and eastern Sudanic Africa, beginning with the Islamic *jihad* or Holy War led by Uthman dan Fodio in Hausaland, northern Nigeria, during the years 1804–9. Uthman claimed to be the forerunner of the Mahdi (the rightly guided one), who would unite the Muslim peoples of the region. In 1881 such a leader appeared in the person of a Sufi holy man named Muhammad Ahmad who, in Kordofan Province, Sudan, declared himself Mahdi. By 1885 he had overthrown the corrupt Turco-Egyptian government in Khartoum and had established the Mahdist state. He died shortly after the fall of Khartoum, and was succeeded by the Khalifa, 'Abd Allah al-Ta'aishi, who was committed

99

The *darawish* (literally 'poor men') or Dervishes, the first followers of the Mahdi, wore ragged tunics of this type, covered with rough, woollen patches. Such tunics (*muraqqaʿa*) had for centuries been the dress of the Sufi religious orders, and signified their contempt for worldly goods. L:91 cm; w:159 cm. 1886,6–28.1.

to perpetuating the ideology of the Mahdiya, a movement of ostensibly religious inspiration, but with revolutionary political and social aims. Mahdism, through the mouthpiece of the Umma party, remains a vital political force in contemporary Sudan.

The followers of the Mahdi were initially drawn predominantly from the *darawish*, literally 'poor men' or religious mendicants, of Kordofan and Darfur. Many were clad in the ragged, patched tunics, *muraqqaʿa*, which, for many centuries, had been the dress of Sufi initiates (Trimingham 1971:181), and signified the rejection of material wealth in embracing the life-style of the religious ascetic. A rare example of a *muraqqaʿa* is in the collections of the British Museum, the year of its registration, 1886, indicating that it was acquired during one of the engagements between the Mahdists and Anglo-Egyptian forces before or shortly after the fall of Khartoum. The base cloth of the tunic is cotton, onto which a number of appliqué 'patches' of coarse, blue woollen cloth have been sewn. It is no coincidence that these patches are made of wool, because it was from this material that the distinctive garments of the early Islamic ascetics who founded the Sufi orders were made, and from which the Sufi derive their name, *suf* being the Arabic for wool.

Although the *darawish*, or Dervishes, gave their allegiance to the Mahdi, they also had loyalties towards their own local shaikhs (religious teachers) and to the particular *tariqa* or order to which each belonged. Clearly this was an unsatisfactory situation for the Mahdi, who saw himself not simply as the initiator of another religious sect, but as the leader of a new World Order. Consequently the Mahdi decreed, after the initial victories of his followers, that they should henceforth be known not as *darawish*, but by the more honourable title of *ansar*, literally 'the helpers', the name given to the men of Medina who supported the Prophet Muhammad (Wingate 1968:48). Furthermore, he commanded that the Dervish orders be abolished and that they should forsake their former religious and tribal affiliations for allegiance to him alone (Trimingham 1949:152). It was at this period that the ragged, home-made *muraqqaʿa* of the *darawish*, which was the original 'uniform' of the Mahdist movement, must have begun to be replaced by an altogether smarter tailored tunic, *jubba*, embellished with symmetrical, appliqué sections of coloured cloth. Significantly, these coloured sections were not made of wool, but usually of cotton.

Among the first to wear the *jubba* were the Baqqara Arabs of Kordofan and Darfur who, after some initial hesitation in joining the *jihad*, had become the backbone of the Mahdist army (Trimingham 1949:153). They made up the bulk of the elite Black Flag division which was commanded by their Amir, ʿAbd Allah, who was destined to become the Khalifa, the Mahdi's successor. By contrast with the poverty of the *darawish*, the Baqqara were comparatively wealthy cattle farmers, many of whom owned their own horses. However, it has been suggested that they lacked the zeal of the *darawish* for the underlying religious inspiration of the Mahdiya, and were motivated more by the prospect of material gain (Holt 1958:118). This new style of *jubba*, of which there are many examples in private and museum collections, was not produced in quantity until a standing army, divided into well-defined tactical units, was established by the Khalifa, as part of his attempt to centralise the Mahdist state. However, by the time of the Battle of Omdurman in 1898, seventeen years after the inception of the Mahdist movement, large numbers of *jubba*, as well as weapons and military equipment of all kinds, were being produced in work-shops specially set up for the purpose (Westerdijk 1988:182, Knight 1986:32, Churchill 1899 vol. 1:125, vol. 2:216, 394).

The distinction, therefore, between the ragged, patched *muraqqa'a* and the more finely tailored and appliquéd *jubba*, cannot simply be explained by the theory, proposed in the pioneering work by Picton and Mack (1989:173), that one was the dress of the rank and file, while the other distinguished the officers in the Mahdist army. Rather, it reflects a subtle, but fundamental, change in the ideology of the Mahdiya. To be sure, the ragged patches and amulet 'pocket' on the *muraqqa'a* of the *darawish* were suggested, in stylised form, on the *jubba* of the *ansar*, thus maintaining a visual metaphor for the religious fervour and ideals which motivated the early days of the Mahdiya. It is also true to say that there were variations, which will be analysed in more detail below, in the *jubba* of the *ansar* which may possibly have denoted military rank or ethnic affiliation. However, the main difference between the two garments is that one was the dress of the *darawish*, the 'poor men', who left their farms to fight for a religious ideal, and returned to the land after the battle to renew their allegiance to the local shaikh or holy man. The other was worn by the *ansar*, who were altogether more ennobled, being named after the original supporters of the Prophet and encouraged to become members of what amounted to a warrior caste, with unswerving and exclusive loyalty to the Mahdi and his successor the Khalifa. On a more secular level, the recognisably defined uniforms of the *ansar* were intended to strengthen the process of centralising the fragmentary Mahdist state by emphasising the authority of the newly formed standing army based in the capital, Omdurman. As such, they were a manifestation of the increasingly militaristic autocracy which characterised the Khalifa's reign. This evolution in the religious and political ideology of the Mahdiya, as reflected in the development of the *jubba*, is also suggested in Churchill's assessment of what he perceived to be the changing motivation of the Mahdist troops at a number of key moments: 'the Arabs who . . . annihilated Hicks fought in the glory of religious zeal; . . . who opposed Graham, Earle and Stewart fought in defence of the soil; . . . who were conquered by Kitchener fought in the pride of an army. Fanatics charged at Shekan; patriots at Abu Klea; warriors at Omdur-man' (1899 vol. 1:60).

Once the *jihad* had been successfully established, the Mahdi began to draw support from a vast area of eastern Sudanic and Central Africa. Many of these widely scattered peoples saw no reason, at least in the early stages of the Mahdiya, to wear the patched *jubba*, preferring instead their own indigenous dress. Typical among such people were the Beja of the Red Sea Province east of the Nile, who were fiercely independent and loyal to their local leaders. The Mahdi sent messengers and detachments of troops to these distant allies, not simply to assist them militarily, but also in an attempt to establish a continuity and consistency in the development of the ideology of the Mahdiya. In this context, wearing the *jubba* would have provided a visible symbol of the authority of the Mahdi for the *ansar* acting on his behalf.

Uthman Diqna was created Amir of the Beja peoples by the Mahdi in 1883, and he was very much responsible for uniting other peoples of the region such as the Bisharin, Beni-Amer and Hadendoa in the Mahdist cause. He was also probably instrumental in encouraging the wearing of the *jubba*, in a distinctive, regional style, among these Red Sea Arabs. The *jubba* most commonly found in

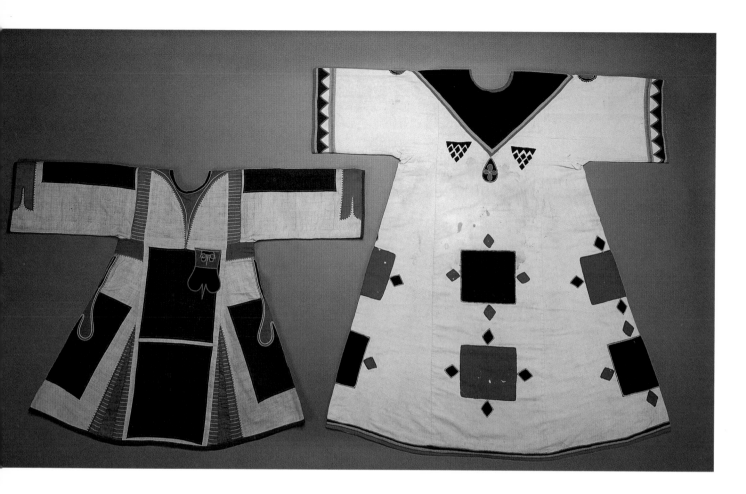

A tunic (*jubba*) with colourful, appliqué panels and pockets, was developed from the ragged Sufi *muraqqa'a* as the 'uniform' of the Mahdists, though in the process it lost much of the religious inspiration which informed the design and appearance of the earlier garment. There were distinct variations in the style and size of *jubba* worn in different regions and by different ethnic groups. The most common was that particularly associated with the Baqqara Arabs (left), who rapidly became the ruling elite in the military autocracy which developed when their leader, the Khalifa, succeeded the Mahdi in 1885. A quite different, and significantly larger, style of *jubba* (right) was worn by the Beja and other Red Sea Arabs who fought for the Mahdist cause, but remained fiercely independent.
L:90 cm; w:125 cm (left). 1972,Af11.14.
L:132 cm; w:131 cm. 1980,Af1.1.

museum collections, although varying considerably in the shape, size, colour and number of their appliquéd sections, are of a particular and easily recognisable type, with common stylistic features. Many were probably produced in the workshops of Omdurman by and for the Baqqara Arabs who dominated the military hierarchy and formed the personal bodyguard of the Khalifa himself. Most of these 'Baqqara' styles of *jubba*, some clearly made for youths and young boys, were inevitably acquired during the campaign which culminated in the final defeat of the Mahdist forces at Omdurman in 1898, and thus probably represent the later developments of this style. A second, and much more unusual, style may be observed on those *jubba* which are not so adroitly tailored and which employ a different range of lozenge-shaped and triangular appliqué motifs. We know of two *jubba* of this type, one in the Royal Marines Museum (Knight 1986:31), the other in the British Museum. Both are attributed to the Beja; in addition, the British Museum example is thought to have belonged to one of the retinue of Uthman Diqna himself. A further piece of evidence which links this style with eastern Sudan may be found in the appliquéd dresses of the Rashaida Arabs of today (see also below), particularly in the style of the serrated, triangular motifs with which both the dresses and the *jubba* are embellished. We may therefore speculate that Uthman Diqna, a resourceful leader, developed this Beja style of *jubba* in order to show solidarity with the Mahdist movement, and yet at the same time to preserve the independent identity of the Beja within this movement.

It has been suggested that the various designs and occasional embroidered motifs on the *jubba* may be insignia of rank. The evidence, however, is inconclusive, and would indicate that it might be misleading to draw too close a parallel between the definition of rank in a Mahdist army and in a comparable Western military hierarchy. The armies of the Mahdist state were divided into four sections, each known as *rub'*, 'a quarter'. These were sub-divided into four further sections, each of which was again divided into four. Amirs of varying seniority commanded the larger divisions, while their immediate subordi-

RIGHT The *jubba* was not only worn by adult men in the Mahdist state, but also by youths and even very young children. L:81 cm; w:89 cm (left). 1949,Af46.692. L:48 cm; w:50 cm. 1945,Af12.8.

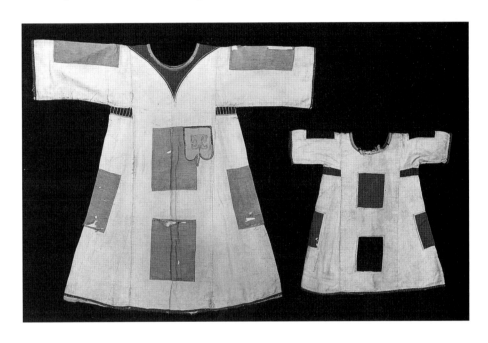

BELOW The Amir Mahmud, who was captured following the battle of Atbara in 1896, wearing a richly patterned *jubba. Photo: Courtesy of the National Army Museum.*

nates, *muqaddam*, were in charge of the smaller units. The smallest subdivisions were commanded by *ru'us mi'at*, literally 'captains of hundreds' (Holt 1958:105,228). Clearly then, there was considerable scope for the use of insignia of some kind to differentiate the various elements of such a hierarchy. Equally clearly, the lowliest *ansar*, though equipped with a *jubba* of considerably more sophisticated cut than the ragged garments of the *darawish*, nonetheless would not have worn the more elaborate designs which are to be found in museum collections. There is also evidence (e.g. the photograph of Amir Mahmud captured at the battle of Atbara, 1896) to show that certain high-ranking Amirs did wear elaborate *jubba*. However, it seems that other Amirs wore *jubba* of a simple design (Gleichen 1905 vol. 1:254). The Khalifa himself is said to have worn a plain white *jubba* (Knight 1986:32, Gleichen 1905 vol. 1:269).

Some *jubba* include small, patch-pockets on the left breast which, it has been suggested, may be insignia of rank, primarily because they are all of the same distinctive shape and are often elaborately embroidered. However, a rough pocket was also sewn onto the *muraqqa'a* of the *darawish* in precisely the same place above the heart, using a piece of material distinctly different from that employed to make the other 'patches'. It is likely that this feature, in common with the ragged 'patches' of the *muraqqa'a*, was also transmitted in stylised form to the *jubba* of the *ansar*. Although there is no known documentary evidence to prove it, these pockets were probably used to hold a talisman, possibly in the form of passages from the Qur'an, to protect the owner from harm. The thin, blade-like design on the lip and in the centre of the lower edge of the pocket, and the star-shaped motifs with which it is often embroidered, are consistent with devices used elsewhere in northern and Sudanic Africa to pierce or otherwise repel the evil eye. For example, the *aska takwas* or 'eight knives' design embroidered on the left breast of Hausa (northern Nigeria) robes may well, in part, fulfil a function of this type.

As a footnote to this discussion of the *muraqqa'a* and the *jubba*, it is interesting to examine how closely they conform with Picton and Mack's observation on the general significance of appliquéd textiles in Africa: 'Where appliquéd cloth is found in Africa, as often as not it is associated with prestige and social position' (1989:169). Undoubtedly the uniform of the *ansar*, even in its simplest form, supports this generalisation. However, it could be argued that, in a subtler way, the ragged *muraqqa'a* of the *darawish* also conforms, in that its intended effect was to confer great religious 'prestige' upon the wearer by visually declaring that he had no secular 'social position' whatsoever. Another common characteristic of the two garments is that, in different ways, they both practise a form of visual deception. The rough 'patches' sewn onto the *muraqqa'a* of the *darawish* do not, in fact, serve to mend tears in the cloth, but instead are intended to emphasise the decrepitude of an already ragged garment. This intention is given visual emphasis by making the patches a different colour to the base cloth. The symmetrical, neatly stitched panels on the *jubba* of the *ansar* are, by contrast, subsumed in the overall design and pattern of the garment, which, interestingly enough, is frequently identical on both 'front' and 'back'. However, although all pretence that they act as repairs to the garment has been dropped, these stylised 'patches' nonetheless retain a suggestion of this particular utilitarian function, with its attendant religious and ideological connotations. Picton and Mack draw an interesting parallel between the Mahdist *jubba* and the appliquéd dance cloths worn by Kuba women of southern Zaire, the intricate patterns of which are thought to have evolved from the shapes of patches used in the mending of cloth. There is, however, a fundamental difference in the motivation which informs the patterning of the two garments, in that the 'patches' on both the *muraqqa'a* and the *jubba* were always intended as a visual metaphor of religious inspiration, and are not derived from a real need to repair the cloth. The patterning on the Kuba skirt, also a visual metaphor in that the 'patches' do not all cover holes, does appear to have been originally inspired by making a virtue out of a functional necessity, namely that of mending tears in the cloth.

Mahdist flags and quilted armour

Flags and banners played an important part in denoting individual sections of the Mahdist army and also, to a certain extent, in announcing the rank and status of those in charge of each group. The army was divided, using geographical and ethnic criteria, into three major sections, each known by the colour of its battle standard. The Black Flag were mainly Western Baqqara Arabs; the Green Flag, predominantly Eastern Baqqara, and the Red Flag were riverain Arabs from the Nile valley (Holt 1958:104). In addition, each Amir or 'commander' had his own particular flag, as did the various auxiliary sections, of differing ethnic affiliation, which joined the regular army in time of battle. These flags displayed exhortations from the Qur'an, and other texts appropriate to the ideology of the Mahdiya, in a script created from appliqué pieces of coloured cloth set on a plain cotton background. Churchill (1899 vol. 2:112)

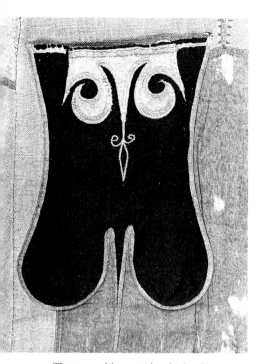

The spear-like motifs which often appear on the patch pockets of the *jubba* may be designed, metaphorically, to pierce the evil eye, and thus negate its harmful effects. The pockets themselves may have contained talismans. L:(of pocket) 19cm; W:12 cm. 1972,Af11.19.

Cotton banner with appliqué border and Arabic script in coloured cloth. Such banners were used to denote individual sections and commands in the Mahdist armies, as well as to boost morale by the exhortations, often from the Qur'an, which they displayed. L:117 cm; W:188 cm. 1953,Af22.1.

describes flags of this type carried by a section of the Khalifa's army at the Battle of Omdurman:

> They could not have mustered less than 6,000. Their array was perfect. They displayed a great number of flags – perhaps 500 – which looked at the distance white, though they were really covered with texts from the Koran, and which by their admirable alignment made this division of the Khalifa's army look like the old representations of the Crusaders in the Bayeux tapestry.

Quilted cotton armour, for the protection of both man and horse, was used across a wide belt of Sudanic Africa from the Niger to the Nile, and is still made today for ceremonial display. However, apart from this specific application, the technique of quilting is not common in the region, or, indeed, anywhere in Africa. Several thicknesses of cloth were sewn together and stuffed with kapok, the wool-like fibre which surrounds the seeds of the silk cotton tree. Some Mahdist cavalrymen wore suits of armour consisting of helmet and coat manufactured from this material, the coat taking the form of a long *jubba*, but with integral, rather than appliquéd, stylised 'patches', usually in red or blue. Their mounts were even more spectacularly attired in a caparison of patchwork quilted armour, sometimes, as in the example in the collections of the British Museum, displaying a dazzling pattern of red, black, yellow and blue triangular sections, and with gold foil strips overlaid. Despite somewhat romantic notions to the contrary, it is unlikely that this type of armour was widely used by the Mahdists in combat, but was probably most often worn at the grand military reviews which were regularly staged at Omdurman.

The Tent Makers of Cairo

Although the craft of the *khiyamiya* or 'tent makers' (from the Arabic *khayma* 'tent') is practised in other Egyptian towns, and, in a similar form, in other countries of the region such as Morocco, it has its heart among the many tiny shops which are located in and around the covered *suq* of Fatimid Cairo which leads to the imposing city gate known as Bab Zuwayla, erected in AD 1092. The Egyptian writer al-Maqrizi, who was born in Cairo in AD 1364, drew on earlier accounts to describe 'The Store of Tents', one of the institutions of Cairo which was linked to the *tiraz* system of the Fatimid period (Serjeant 1948:112–13):

> Among the articles brought forth from the treasuries of al-Kasr, was a countless number of packages containing tents, large tents, tents with two poles, flat-roofed tents, military tents, fortress tents, and castle tents, tents with one side only, pavilions and marquees manufactured of Dabiki and velvet stuffs, Khusrawani stuffs, royal brocade, Armenian stuff, cloth from Bahnasa and Karduwan (in Persia), and the best kind of Halabi (stuff manufactured at Aleppo [Syria]) . . . of various colors and kinds . . . embroidered with designs of elephants, wild beasts, horses, peacocks, birds and other kinds of wild animals, and human beings . . . of all manner of striking and wonderful forms and shapes.

Working in the great tent lofts above the *suq* leading to Bab Zuwayla, the tent makers of Cairo have, for many generations, created from appliquéd scraps of cloth the arabesque-patterned hanging panels which adorn large tents, *suradiq* or *siwan*, erected to accommodate people at important events. Commissions are received through a middleman or agent, *farrash*, who rents to the customer the material required to construct and decorate a *siwan*.

The covered 'street of the tentmakers' in Fatimid Cairo. *Photo: C. Spring.*

Appliqué patterned hangings strung between lamp posts and rolled up on transverse poles spanning a street in Cairo. In the evening they will be fully unfurled to form a tent which will accommodate the mourners at a funeral. *Photo: C. Spring.*

Tent making has always been the stock-in-trade of the *khiyamiya*, but they can turn their hand to producing cloths of virtually any size and pattern that the customer requires. Cushion covers are a popular option, produced with the tourist market in mind. However, they also provide the tent makers with an opportunity to produce individual motifs of the type which, when repeated many times in combination with other elements of the design, make up the composite patterns characteristic of the larger hanging panels of the *siwan*. Far from being a manifestation of the decadence of the craft of the *khiyamiya*, these cushion covers should rather be seen as artists' preliminary sketches, by means of which a vast range of elements may be tested for possible inclusion in a broader canvas.

106

Three main categories of design predominate among the products of the *khiyamiya*. Firstly, arabesques, in a wide variety of different patterns and colours; secondly, decorative Arabic scripts, being mainly quotations from the Qur'an; finally, Pharaonic scenes and other folkloric images geared almost exclusively to the tourist market. The tent makers' clientele also includes people from other Arab countries whose tastes may differ considerably from their Egyptian customers. For example, they make hangings for Saudi Arabians which tend to be far more subdued than those commonly seen in Egypt, predominantly employing darker colours, particularly green, the colour associated with the Prophet Muhammad. The Pharaonic scenes, while un-

A tent maker, working in his tiny shop in the *suq al-khiyamiya*, carefully sews a piece of coloured material to fit the design already drawn onto the canvas base of the cloth he is making.
Photo: C. Spring.

doubtedly made mainly for sale to visitors, are neither, as is sometimes suggested, a particularly recent 'line' of the *khiyamiya*, nor another example of declining standards. Certainly they were being produced in the early twentieth century, probably in response to the stimulus gained through archaeological finds. The discovery of the tomb of Tutankhamun in 1922 would undoubtedly have initiated a further demand for such work. However, the slump in visitors to Egypt following the Gulf War and the subsequent political unrest will simply have served as a reminder of how fickle a market tourism can be. The *khiyamiya* have been in business far too long ever to rely solely on one source of custom.

Today, factory-printed cloth, imitating the designs produced by the *khiyamiya*, may be seen everywhere in the major cities of Egypt. Whether this

ABOVE Cushion cover with arabesque design in appliqué blue cotton. L:89 cm; w:89 cm. 1993,Af24.15.

cloth is having an adverse effect on the craft of the tent maker is a debatable point. Unlike the canvas-backed, appliquéd hangings, it fades rapidly and is easily torn. The fact that the poorest stall holder can now have a piece of *khiyamiya*-inspired cloth on the front of his barrow does not mean that he is a customer lost to the tent makers themselves. The cost of the genuine article would always have been beyond the pocket of such citizens. In fact, almost any manufacturing industry will attest that a proliferation of imitations increases rather than reduces the demand for 'the real thing'.

The craft of the *khiyamiya* is a family concern, the older male members normally being the master craftsmen who draw or trace the intricate designs onto a canvas base. It is said that these designs were once exclusively drawn by hand, though today many of the more intricate examples are created on a large paper template to achieve geometrical accuracy. An element of the design is drawn onto the paper which may then be folded many times depending on the complexity of the pattern, the same element being duplicated on each occasion. The design on the completed template is then perforated with tiny holes (Feeny 1986:23) and secured to the base cloth. Carbon powder is brushed gently through the holes, leaving a pattern on the cloth beneath, which can later be

A screen of factory-printed, *khiyamiya*-inspired cloth, set up at a street café in Cairo. *Photo: C. Spring.*

enhanced with a soft pencil. Younger apprentices, using scissors, needle and thread, then sew pieces of coloured cotton cloth to precisely cover individual motifs. Each piece is at first cut only roughly to the shape of the particular design element it is intended to cover. As the craftsman progresses, he trims and crimps the edge of the scrap of material with a series of small cuts before tucking it underneath and sewing it with invisible stitches to fit exactly the design on the base cloth. The crimping ensures that no unsightly folds or bumps appear beneath the surface of the appliqué sections.

It may only be a coincidental connection with the craft of the *khiyamiya* practised close by, but there has long been a belief that the ancient wooden door of Bab Zuwayla has healing properties. In hope of being cured, the sick and infirm still sometimes come to attach to the gate scraps of their clothing which have been in contact with their afflicted bodies (Ammoun 1991:54).

Embroidery

It is the cultural significance of textiles rather than the technical means of their production which is the main focus of this book, though sometimes, of course, the two are indivisible. In the case of embroidery, the types of stitches used in North Africa are relatively limited, being confined mainly to running or flat, rather than the more complex looped, knotted or chain varieties (Stone 1985:196). The results, however, are remarkable, and examples chosen to illustrate other chapters in this book demonstrate the variety and virtuosity of the textiles embellished by this means.

Embroidery is largely an urban craft in North Africa, particularly in Ethiopia and in the Maghrib countries of Morocco, Algeria and Tunisia. As such, it

Dress (*jubba matruza*) from the village of Hammamet, Tunisia. It is embroidered with gold thread, and further embellished with a thick plait of passementerie gold braid and silk on the bodice. Different elements of the embroidery suggest Andalusian and Ottoman influences. L:93 cm; w:60 cm. 1990,Af18.1.

Woman's cotton dress from Bahriya Oasis in the Western Desert of Egypt. It is embroidered with coloured cotton and coins, both real and imitation, in the Bahriyan style. The cotton fringes on the shoulders and beneath the bodice are also characteristic of the dresses of Bahriya. L:124 cm; W:135 cm. 1978,Af15.1.

reflects, to a greater extent than the weaving tradition, the historical influences which have shaped the cultural development of the region. It was in the great towns that immigrant craftspeople settled. Jews, Andalusians, Turks and Armenians all contributed to the dynamism of existing traditions by the introduction of their own repertoire of skills, echoes of which are still clearly recognisable, particularly in the distinctive embroideries for which certain towns such as Fes, Algiers and Hammamet became famous. We use the term 'embroidery' here in its broadest possible application, for some of the crafts do not conform strictly to the technique of embellishing a ready-woven cloth simply by means of needle and thread. Included in this broader definition are skills such as passementerie, which involves the embellishment of a base cloth or a tailored costume with bands, braids and plaits, often of gold or another metallic thread. Fine examples of this technique may be found on the dresses, *jubba matruza*, of Hammamet, on the coast of Tunisia, which boast a thick, horseshoe-shaped plait of gold thread and blue silk on the bodice. There is a remarkable resemblance between the winged shoulders of this dress, stiffened with heavy gold braid, and a similar feature displayed on the Spanish matador's 'suit of lights'. In addition to this suggestion of a possible Andalusian influence in the design of the dress, it has also been observed (Stone 1985:133) that there is a similarity between the technique of embroidery on the rest of the dress and that employed on Turkish 'towels'. The *jubba matruza* is cited here as just one example of the range of techniques and cross-cultural influences reflected in the embroidered textiles of the Maghrib countries. However, there are many other distinctive styles and techniques of embroidery characteristic of certain regions and towns of North Africa, some of which are examined elsewhere in this book.

Embroidered sleeves and bodice of a married woman's dress from Dakhla Oasis in the Western Desert of Egypt, quite possibly produced in the village of Qalamun. Note the nursing slit below the right arm. L(of dress): 130 cm; w:151 cm. 1991,Af23.21.

Cloak of brown cotton worn by married women of the Rashaida of eastern Sudan. It is embellished with geometric patterns produced by numerous metal staples, which gives the impression of more conventional embroidery. L:158 cm; W:124 cm. 1978,Af19.2.

In the rural regions of Tunisia, Sudan and particularly Egypt, embroidery of a quite different style to the sophisticated finery of urban North Africa may be found. In the Chenini district of Tunisia, small, woollen shawls (*katfiya*) are used by married women as shoulder-cloths, in order to prevent excess oil applied to the hair from staining their dresses. The *katfiya* are frequently embellished with resist-dyed patterns, and with simple embroidery.

In eastern Sudan, another form of embroidery may be seen on the clothes of the married women of the transhumant Rashaida people, who wear a cloak, face veil and colourful, appliquéd cotton dress. The dress is noted above as having stylistic similarities to the Mahdist *jubba* thought to have been worn by peoples from this region. The veil and cloak, by contrast, are of plain, dark brown cotton, but 'embroidered' in intricate patterns produced by clipping thousands of tiny, white metal staples through the base cloth in a way which resembles embroidery stitches.

In the oases of the Western Desert of Egypt, the practice of embellishing wedding dresses represents the most complex and widespread tradition of what we term 'rural embroidery' within the region (Rugh 1986:53–71; Mehrez 1993:4–5; Vivian 1990:45,89–90,145–6; Ammoun 1991:8–11). The spectacular dresses of Siwa Oasis have been discussed in detail elsewhere in this book. Suffice it to say that the style of embroidery, usually in orange, green and red rayon (formerly silk), which embellishes Siwan dresses and a range of other garments including shawls, trousers and shoes, is uniquely different from that of the other oases of the Western Desert such as Bahriya, Dakhla and Kharga. The latter style, though highly distinctive in its own way, is nonetheless recognisably linked to the embroidery found on the dresses of Palestine and of Northern Sinai. Married women's dresses of the Western Desert, with the exception of those of Siwa, are of black cotton shirting imported from the Nile valley, and are traditionally embroidered with complex panels of overlapping cotton cross-stitches around the bodice and lower part of the back, the rest of the dress being usually embellished with relatively simple linear patterns of embroidery. The decoration of the bodice was once mainly augmented with rows of old 5 piastre pieces, and, more recently, with imitation coins made in the Nile valley, which are scarcely more than sequins stamped with a simple design. Many dresses display a combination of real and imitation coins. Each oasis has its own distinct style and colouring of dress, and, until recently, individual villages within the same oasis produced recognisable sub-styles. Today, this complex style of embroidery is little practised, and the dresses which display it are predominantly worn by older women. During the last few decades, improved transport and telecommunications have brought the oases closer to the Nile valley, making imported and manufactured goods much more freely available.

The dresses of Bahriya are exemplified by rectangular sections, outlined by coins, on either side of and immediately below the neck opening, and with a central, rectangular panel on the chest. Another distinctively Bahriyan feature is the inclusion of rows of tassels at the shoulders and along the lower edge of the central panel. In general, the designs of Bahriya dresses tend to be less conservative than those of Farafra, Dakhla and Kharga oases, often including elements which are a departure from the norm and represent the taste of an individual embroideress. The colours also tend to be more varied than on the dresses of other oases, including red, yellow, brown, green, purple and orange

A married woman of Bahriya Oasis, in Egypt's Western Desert, carrying water bottles. She wears a dress, the bodice of which is embroidered in a style unique to Bahriya. The photograph was probably taken in the early 1940s. *Photo: A. Fakhry, courtesy of the American University in Cairo Press.*

embroidered stitching, sometimes incorporated on the same dress (Fakhry 1974:41). The use of a wider spectrum of colours may have been stimulated by the relative proximity of Cairo to the east, and the consequently greater availability of a variety of dyed yarns, or, perhaps, by the influence of Siwa to the west, with its own colourful and highly individual tradition of embroidery. At least one village in Bahriya is predominantly populated by people of Siwan origin (Fakhry 1974:21).

The dresses of Dakhla and Kharga are more restrained, both in variety of design and in the preference for darker purple, blue and red embroidery yarn. This is not to say that the dresses of these oases are not as beautiful as those of Bahriya, or that they do not display the same skill in embroidery. Within Dakhla Oasis it is still possible to distinguish several separate styles of embroidery which are characteristic of the villages of Balat, Qalamun, Bashindi and Mushiya. A typical Balat dress has a square, embroidered bodice embellished with buttons and coins, not unlike that of Bahriya, but without an embroidered central panel on the chest. The dresses of Bashindi and Mushiya both have large, pointed, heavily embroidered central panels embellished with numerous coins, although that of Bashindi is somewhat longer and narrower than that of Mushiya. In common with all Dakhla dresses, they have extensive, embroidered panels on the lower back. The Qalamun dress has the squared bodice which is common to all Dakhla dresses, but its pointed, central panel is formed from as many as six separate lines of embroidery, one inside the other, which extend up to the neck opening, the shape of the panel being further emphasised by several rows of coins.

Pair of resist-dyed cloths (*katfiya*) worn across the shoulders by Berber women in the Chenini district, southern Tunisia. These cloths are designed to protect women's dresses from excess oil in the hair. The circular patterns are created by tying small objects into the cloth before dyeing, whereas the white patterns are embroidered in cotton.
L:85 cm; w:33 cm (left). 1973, Af28.5.
L:92 cm; w:41 cm. 1973,Af28.1.

The embroidery of dresses from Kharga Oasis is quite different again from that of either Bahriya or Dakhla. The embroidery is much less dense, as is the distribution of attached coins, and does not emphasise the bodice or central panel with the same forcefulness. However, the frontal panel, consisting of thin, vertical lines interspersed with small, separate motifs at regular intervals, reaches almost to the hem, quite unlike that on other oasis dresses, which does not normally extend below the waist. It is possible, because of Kharga's proximity to the Nile valley, that these designs have been influenced by the technique of embroidery using metallic thread known as *telli* which was once commonplace on many of the dresses of Upper Egypt.

Resist Dyeing

In Africa, the practice of producing a pattern on ready-woven cloth by the use of dye in combination with a resisting agent is generally associated with the sub-Saharan region, and with coastal West Africa in particular. However, this technique is used among certain Berber peoples of the Maghrib countries of North Africa, and seems to have been more widely practised in the early

114

twentieth century (Ricard 1925:411–26). The method of using starch or wax as the resisting agent, as used by the Yoruba of Nigeria for example, is unknown in North Africa, where the technique is, with one exception, confined to that of 'tie and dye'.

In Morocco, Berber women of the Ayt Atta and Djebala peoples produce, respectively, tie-dyed head coverings and belts displaying simple, two-tone, circular patterns. These are achieved by first dyeing the base cloth yellow or some other light colour, and then by tying some resistant twine, such as a sliver of palm leaf, around an object, large or small depending on the pattern required. Finally, the bound cloth is soaked in a bath of dark dye before being removed, untied and washed to reveal the pattern.

Much more sophisticated are the resist-dyed cloths which were produced in the Gharyan region of Libya (Ricard 1925:416–19), displaying concentric circles of patterns of varying complexity, the simplest of which was achieved by tying up a tiny bunch of cloth containing a single grain of wheat in the way described above. This pattern was enlarged by the simple expedient of extending the twine to gather in a larger bunch of cloth beneath the bound grain of wheat. In the centre of these Gharyan textiles, an intricate pattern was produced by tying seven individual grains in the same way, and then gathering the cloth beneath the group thus created, before winding palm leaf twine in a tight spiral around the bunched cloth. Hundreds of tightly bound bundles, each containing a grain of wheat, would be painstakingly created in these various ways before the entire textile was submerged in a dye bath. The choice of a grain of wheat, as opposed to a pebble or some other small object, is of significance because wheat was considered to be particularly imbued with *baraka*.

Another example of the use of sophisticated resist-dye techniques is provided by the shoulder coverings (*katfiya*), which are produced in the Chenini district surrounding the town of Gabes in southern Tunisia (Vivier 1995:106, 112). The base cloth is of woven wool, with a row of tassels at each end. Also at each end are simple patterns embroidered on the cloth using cotton. The cloths are then tied and dyed in a similar way to that described above, except that they are dipped and re-tied several times to achieve a multicoloured pattern. The tassels may also be tie-dyed or individually dyed in a variety of colours. Small, circular patterns are produced by tying a few grains of wheat in each small bundle. Crumpling the cloth at both ends achieves a gradual lightening of the colour from the centre outwards. Finally, the embroidered motifs in cotton, which do not take up the dye readily absorbed by the wool base cloth, stand out in white on the now dark background. This latter technique is, as far as we know, unique in the African resist-dyeing tradition, and reaches its finest expression in the patterning of head-coverings such as the *bakhnuq*, and the *ta'jira*. These cloths are woven on the upright, single-heddle Berber loom, predominantly using plain, undyed white woollen yarn, though occasionally black wool is employed (Reswick 1981:64). The complex, supplementary weft patterns characteristic of these textiles are, however, of cotton, woven into the woollen base cloth using the technique of tapestry weaving. It is not difficult to imagine the skill required to weave these designs in white on a background of virtually the same colour. Subsequent to weaving, the entire cloth is dyed, then washed, leaving the white weft patterns of cotton sharply defined on a coloured background.

Diagram showing the way in which grains of wheat are tied into numerous bunches, using palm fibre strips, to produce the complex patterns found on the resist-dyed cloths of the Gharyan region, Libya. From P. Ricard *Le Batik Berbere*, Hespéris, 1925, p. 418.

Plaiting and Knitting

Plaited woollen yarn is a familiar and widespread feature within the canon of North African textile crafts. It may, for example, form the additional tassels which embellish woven cloth, costume and accoutrements. Alternatively, it is used to fashion the decorative bands which secure the head-dresses worn by Berber women in the High Atlas mountains of Morocco, the belts worn by Tunisian women in El-Jem (Tanfous 1971:103) and the various tresses for the hair worn by women throughout the region. The requirement to conceal the hair after marriage is an important factor in the production of these tresses,

Woollen, plaited bands (left) of the type worn by women of the Atlas mountains, Morocco, and woollen plaits (right), with small purses attached, worn by women of Bahriya Oasis, Egypt. L:125 cm; w:190 cm (Morocco). 1969,Af37.7–8. L:84 cm; L:82 cm (Egypt). 1991, Af23.4–5.

reaching perhaps its most elaborate expression in the spectacular, plaited wedding 'wigs' of Ghadames Oasis, western Libya.

In the oases of the Western Desert of Egypt, plaited tresses of various designs and materials, known as '*uqus* in Bahriya (Fakhry 1974:42) and *rashrash* in Dakhla, are still made and worn by women on the back of the head and interwoven with their natural hair. They are practically identical to those described by Lane (1871 vol. 2:324):

. . . it is the general practice of the women of these classes to divide their hair into only two tresses behind, and to plait, with each of these tresses, three red silk strings, each of which has a tassel at the end, and reaches more than half-way

Knitted woollen hat and trousers (*tha 'ban*). Children of Farafra Oasis in Egypt's Western Desert wear hats of this type. The trousers are worn by hunters of the Ayt Oumalou of the High Atlas mountains of Morocco during the cold, winter season. This particular pair was clearly knitted in 1968. Knitting is an exclusively male activity in the rural areas of North Africa. L:20 cm; w:23 cm (hat). 1991,Af23.8.L:117 cm; w:55 cm. 1969,Af37.25.

towards the ground, so that they are usually obliged to draw aside the tassels before they sit down. These appendages are called *'okoos*.

Older examples of *'uqus* in Bahriya tend to be made of thick cotton or silk thread, naturally dyed; more recently, aniline-dyed knitting wool has become popular. Sometimes a combination of the two materials is used. The designs vary in complexity, but are invariably composed of three strands knotted together at the top. The simplest is a single plait with a tassel at the end, with perhaps a few base metal rings encircling the plait just above the tassel. The more complex strands may include padded, sausage-shaped sections which split into three or more individual plaits, each one ending in a padded bobble. Often small amulets, to ward off the evil eye, sequins, or little cloth purses for money are attached to the *'uqus*.

It is common practice among the Berber peoples of North Africa for men to cut up and tailor the cloth woven by women, and to produce the additional plaited tassels with which a variety of textile-based objects are embellished. Men of the Zayan people of central Morocco cut up hand-woven, tapestry-patterned woollen cloth, and sew it into a number of items including boots, pillows and, in particular, decorative saddlebags which are used for carrying gunpowder and other accessories during the *fantasia* (Forelli and Harries 1977:45), the annual festival celebrating the founder of the first Moroccan dynasty, Maulay Idris. These saddlebags, *smatt*, are further embellished with numerous decorative tassels. The prestige afforded to the owner of the most ostentatious saddlebag makes their creation a matter of fiercely competitive pride among the young men of the Zayan.

Finally we should mention that knitted garments are occasionally produced in the region, and always by men. The brown and white striped trousers (*tha'ban*) worn by hunters of the Ayt Oumalou of the High Atlas (Morocco) are knitted from natural wool as a protection against the cold winters of the region (Besancenot 1990:158). In the quite different environment of Farafra oasis in Egypt's Western Desert, men also knit articles of clothing, including strong white gloves and colourful children's hats.

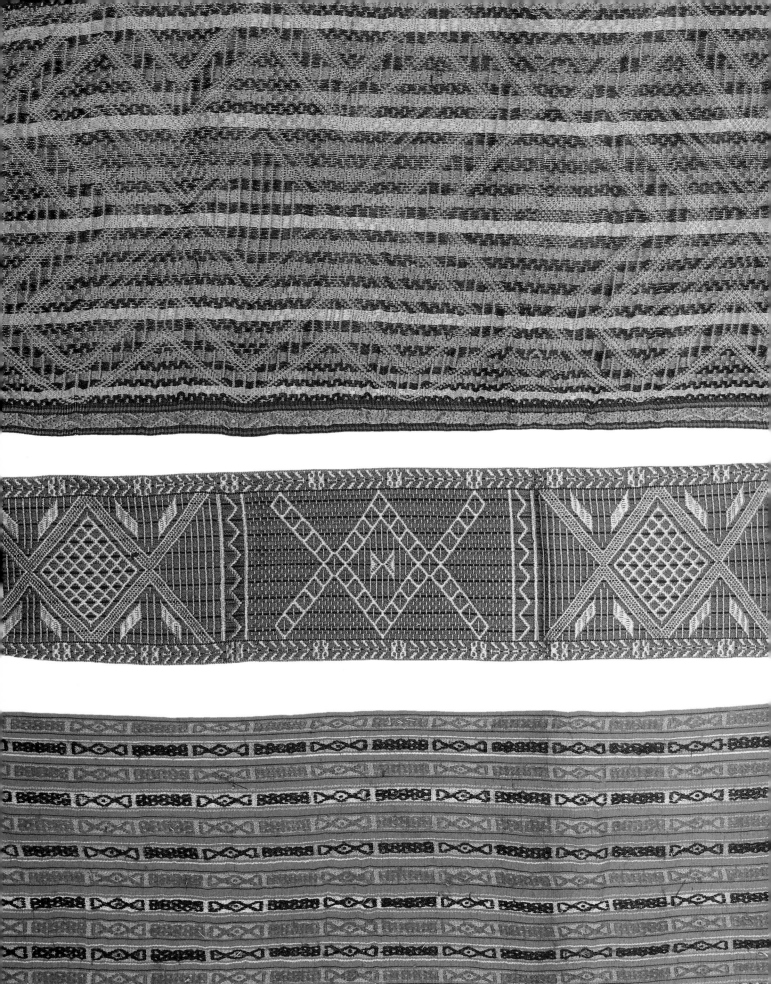

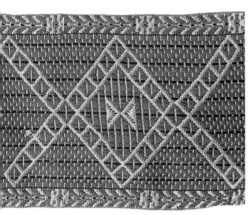

7

SECULAR AND SACRED

THE TEXTILES OF ETHIOPIA

Ethiopia is undoubtedly the most important centre for the production of handmade cloth in Eastern Africa, and has always held this position of pre-eminence. As in other parts of Africa, the textile tradition in Ethiopia has shown itself to be supremely resilient, dynamic and adaptable to change. Despite the vicissitudes of war, famine and political upheavals, and in the face of the competition posed by machine technology, imported goods, changing life-styles and foreign fashions, the volume of handmade textiles produced in Ethiopia has probably never been greater than in the latter half of the twentieth century.

The technical aspects of cloth production in Ethiopia – the raw materials, their preparation and the types of loom commonly used – are dealt with in some detail in Chapter 2 of this book. This chapter examines the significance of textiles in Ethiopian culture.

During the first millennium BC a powerful kingdom developed in Ethiopia with its capital at Aksum in the northern province of Tegré. Early in the fourth century AD, this kingdom was converted to Christianity and remained the focus of religious, political and military power in Ethiopia until the eleventh century. Thereafter, the more southerly provinces of Lasta and Shawa assumed

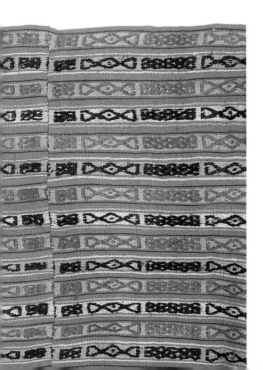

Three different patterned borders (*tibeb*) of silk and rayon incorporated in the wraparound cotton shawl (*shamma*). Shawls with a multicoloured and elaborately patterned silk band became more widely worn by the elite of Ethiopian society during the late nineteenth century, replacing a type with a single red band which had been fashionable wear for well-to-do men and women up until that time. Such shawls were ultimately used as shrouds for the dead. Today the *tibeb* is woven in rayon, in a wide variety of designs, and it may be worn by a still wider cross-section of society. L:235 cm; W:143 cm (top – entire cloth). 1974, Af11.5. L:81 cm; W:14 cm (border only). 1969, Af33.1. L:242 cm; W:170 cm. 1912, 4–10. 35.

119

A gathering of high-ranking ecclesiastical officials to celebrate Temqat (Epiphany), near Aksum in Tegré province. Note the elaborately embroidered cape (*lamd*), with pendent panels, worn by the enthroned priest in the centre of the picture. The woman in the foreground is wearing a cotton shawl (*shamma*) with a silk or rayon patterned border (*tibeb*). *Photo: J. Phillips.*

increasing importance, though Tegré, with its mountainous terrain and access to Red Sea ports, remained a powerful kingdom. In 1632 a permanent capital of the Christian empire of the northern and central highlands was established at Gondar. The power of the emperor was, however, dictated by the amount of allegiance shown to him by the rulers of numerous and, at times, virtually independent kingdoms. It was not until the mid-nineteenth century that the first of a succession of enlightened emperors began truly to unify the country.

Until the beginning of the twentieth century the pattern of textile production in Ethiopia must have remained virtually unchanged. In the large towns, guilds of specialist weavers, embroiderers and tailors worked under the protection and patronage of the powerful ecclesiastical and politico-military elites, producing for them the garments which helped to define rank and status within a complex and strictly defined hierarchical society. Other groups of weavers would have produced the cloth from which the costume of the urban population was made, with pattern, colour and fineness of weave again indicating status and class. In rural areas, weavers worked mainly to satisfy local, predominantly utilitarian, demands, though would also make garments of ritual significance to their particular ethnic groups. By the turn of the century, with travel made safer within a unified empire, rural weavers began the practice of seasonal migration to large towns during certain periods of the year when good profits were to be made. Many of the weavers to be found in Addis Ababa today, for example, are Dorze people from the Gamu Gofa highlands in southern Ethiopia. The seasonal presence of weavers in smaller towns may correspond with another type of economic activity such as coffee growing. The larger towns of Sidamo province in southern Ethiopia experience an influx of weavers from rural areas when the coffee crop is harvested and processed, at which time a ready market is available for the sale of cloth (Karsten 1972:94).

Weavers are often part of an ethnic or religious minority within the commu-

A Muslim craftsman of Aksum, in Tegré province, weaving a prestigious, multicoloured border of complex pattern (*tibeb*) into a toga-like shawl (*shamma*) the garment which is worn by men and women throughout Ethiopia. *Photo: S. Bell.*

nities among which they work. In addition to the Dorze weavers in Addis Ababa already mentioned, Muslims monopolise the craft in northern towns such as Aksum (Bell, personal correspondence), while Falashas (Ethiopian Jews), historically at least, were responsible for the production of many fine textiles in the area of Gondar (Pankhurst 1964:224). There is evidence, both historical and contemporary, to suggest that weavers suffer to a certain extent from social discrimination. Among the Christian Amhara peoples of the northern and central highlands, weavers are considered to be among those people, together with blacksmiths and potters, who have the power to cast the evil eye on other members of the community (Reminick 1976:86–7). However, prejudice may not simply be against the craftspeople themselves and their perceived ethnic minority status, but also against the raw material they use and the processes employed to fashion it into the finished product. In the southern provinces of the country, raw cotton and cotton yarn are still viewed as dangerous, powerful substances, and white as the colour of death. Yet in this region of Ethiopia little discrimination against weavers was detected during research in the 1970s, except among the Konso (Karsten 1972:113–4) – and even in Konso society it was noted that attitudes had softened and prejudice had diminished considerably in recent years (Hallpike 1972:140). In the past, discrimination of this type resulted in certain crafts remaining the monopoly of particular groups within the community for many generations, and one can point to a similar pattern in other parts of Africa, particularly with regard to blacksmiths. Such differentiation was not, of course, always to the disadvantage of the craftspeople themselves, and in some cases was positively encouraged by them, particularly in a society where most family groups were otherwise virtually self-sufficient in material goods, as they were in many parts of Ethiopia until relatively recently. Thus the diminution of prejudice against weavers in Ethiopia during the late twentieth century may not simply be explained by the increasing liberal-mindedness of society, but also by the fact

121

that in some cases it may no longer be within the economic interests of the weaver to perpetuate the way in which he was once perceived by the rest of the community.

Cloth, Class and Communication: the Ethiopian *shamma*

The varieties of wrap-around, toga-like shawls worn by both men and women in Ethiopia are collectively known as *shamma*, but each type has its own name and distinctive use. All are composed of two or more thicknesses of the muslin-like cotton cloth woven by hand in many parts of Ethiopia. Some have no decoration whatsoever, others have a plain coloured border, *limut*, along one edge. Still others boast a multicoloured band, *tibeb*, with numerous supplementary weft patterns in silk or rayon. The broader and more complex the *tibeb*, the more prestigious the *shamma*.

There are three principal types of *shamma*, though it must be remembered that even within these broad categories there are variations denoted by the fineness of the weave, the type of material used, and the size, colour and complexity of the *tibeb*. The *natala* is a lightweight shawl, usually composed of two thicknesses of cotton cloth, and worn by men in the summer months and by women as an essential complement to the cotton dress, *kamis*. The *kutta* is a larger and heavier cloth, while the *buluko* is larger still. Both are worn as a sleeping blanket at night or, in colder weather, during the day. Ultimately, they may be used as a shroud for the dead. Mansfield Parkyns (1853 vol 2:10–11) describes the former use while suggesting the latter:

A bachelor rolls himself up in his cloth – head, feet, face, and all completely covered up. Married couples sleep in the same manner; that is quite naked, but rolled up close together in a sort of hydropathic dry pack, or double mummy fashion.

Today the *shamma* is worn, in one form or another, by most of the Ethiopian peoples, though it was once more characteristic of the northern and central highlands. Ethiopian society, both urban and rural, religious and secular, has long been structured upon a complex hierarchy of rank and status. Dress is one way of defining and demonstrating this gradation, and the *shamma*, worn by such a large percentage of the population, has always been an important instrument in this process.

Mid-nineteenth century sources (Lefebvre 1845–8) suggest that at this time a *shamma* with a plain red border was worn by both men and women of the aristocracy as a sign of status, certainly in Tegré province in the northern highlands. Parkyns (1853 vol 2:7–8) also describes this red-bordered *shamma*, which he refers to as a 'quarry', as well as a type of very fine *shamma* with a multicoloured silk border which he calls a 'mergeff':

The 'quarry' is the principal article of Abyssinian dress: it is of cotton, and very fine and soft; those of the richer being finer but probably not so serviceable as those of the poorer class. It is made in three pieces; each piece is about three feet broad by fifteen long. Near both ends of each piece is a red stripe, five or six inches broad. To sew the three pieces together, one is first taken and doubled carefully, so that the red stripes of each come exactly together. A second piece is then taken, and also folded, but inside out, and one half of it laid under and the other half over the first piece, so that the four red borders now come together. One edge of this quadruple cloth is then sewn from top to bottom, and the last mentioned piece is turned back, so that the two together form one double cloth of two breadths. The third piece is now added in a similar manner, and the whole forms a "quarry" which . . . is a white double cloth, with a red border near the bottom only; the breadth of the 'quarry' is nine feet by seven and a half long. An inferior quality of this cloth is made of much coarser material, and without a stripe . . . The lower class and working people wear these inferior cloths stitched together on common occasions, and perhaps have for Sunday best a cheap 'quarry' with a blue stripe. But above all is the 'mergeff', a sort of cloth made after the fashion of the first-mentioned one, but of such fineness that it requires to be of six pieces instead of three to give it sufficient body, and is worn quadruple instead of double. Its stripe or border is of red, yellow, and blue silk, neatly worked together instead of plain red cotton. Such an article of finery is, of course, worn only by ladies and some few great men.

As in the case of silk weavers in other parts of Africa, such as the Asante of Ghana, the Ethiopian *tibeb* weavers first obtained their supplies of yarn from imported cloths which they unravelled. Also in common with the Asante *kente* cloth and the *lamba* woven by the Merina of Madagascar, the silk *tibeb* of the Ethiopian *shamma* displayed an increasing variety and complexity of pattern and colour towards the end of the nineteenth century. By the turn of the century, the fine *shammas* which Parkyns described as being the prerogative of only a very few were beginning to be worn by larger numbers of well-to-do members of society. This gradual relaxation of the rules governing the wearing of particular types of cloth continued as the twentieth century progressed. As supplies of synthetic yarn such as rayon, which has some of the qualities of silk, also became more widely available, the *tibeb* weavers found an increasing market for their craft, to the extent that today a client may choose from dozens of different patterns and colours. The complexity and width of the *tibeb* is still, however, very much an indication of status, and the *tibeb* weavers themselves

Mid-nineteenth-century illustration showing a type of *shamma* with a red border being worn by a courtier (left) and a church lawyer. The way in which the *shamma* is draped can communicate the mood and attitude of the wearer. The courtier is showing deference to a superior, whereas the lawyer is walking, in relaxed mood, in the street. From T. Lefebvre, *Voyage en Abyssinie*, Paris 1845–8.

enjoy a superior status to others of their craft who can only weave plain cotton or *limut* (cloth with a monochrome border).

Although the type and the quality of the *shamma* conveys certain information about the wearer, the precise way in which this garment is worn communicates a further and equally important range of data. Subtle variations of mood, attitude and intention may be reflected without recourse to speech. This use of the *shamma* was noted by at least one commentator of the mid-nineteenth century (Lefebvre 1845–8:1,28) and was observed and recorded by another (Messing 1960:558–61) over a century later. At least a dozen different and non-utilitarian ways of wearing the *shamma*, among both men and women, were identified, including those denoting assurance, sadness, reserve, self-abasement and respect.

Women's Wear: the development of the *kamis* dress

Women's dress in Ethiopia in many ways resembles that of men. Both sexes wear the *shamma*, though women tend to wear the lighter and smaller *natala* as an essential complement to the dress, *kamis* (from the French chemise), in its various forms. Both sexes also may wear a cotton tunic and wide-waisted, jodhpur-style trousers which are tight fitting around the calf, though the latter were, and still are, only worn by women of the aristocracy or urban elite. Parkyns (1853 vol. 2:25) describes the mid-nineteenth century dress of the women of Tegré province thus:

An ordinary woman wears a large, loose shirt down to the feet, with sleeves made tight towards the wrist. This with a 'quarry' [*shamma*] similar to those of the men, but worn rather differently, and a parasol when out of doors, is a complete suit. A fine lady, however, has a splendid 'mergeff quarry' [*shamma* with multicoloured,

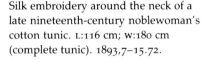

Silk embroidery around the neck of a late nineteenth-century noblewoman's cotton tunic. L:116 cm; w:180 cm (complete tunic). 1893,7–15.72.

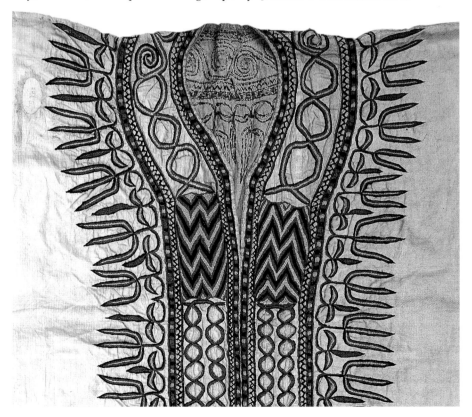

Embroidery around the ankle of a pair of lady's trousers made in Addis Ababa in 1993. Such work is now executed by male craftsmen. L:105 cm; w:41 cm (trousers). 1993,Af16.2b.

patterned border in silk] as before described, and her shirt is made probably of calico from Manchester, instead of the country fabric, and richly embroidered in silk of divers and various patterns round the neck, down the front, and on the cuffs.

The preference for making these tunics out of machine-made cotton shirting from Manchester, probably as much because it provided a better base for fine embroidery than for any prestige value it might have, is an interesting historical footnote. Another example of the stimulus given to an indigenous craft by the availability of such cotton cloth may be seen in its use as an efficient base for the resist-dyed indigo *adire* cloth of the Yoruba of Nigeria which developed rapidly during the twentieth century.

Parkyns goes on to describe the embroidered trousers of Ethiopian noblewomen in a tone which reflects his amused abhorrence of a fashion just beginning to be worn by a handful of English women: 'She . . . may choose to wear (alas, that it should be so even in Abyssinia!) the inexpressibles. These are made of calico, and rather loose, but getting gradually tighter at the ankle, where they are embroidered like the shirt.'

During the nineteenth and early twentieth centuries, embroidery of this type was a fashionable and acceptable pursuit for Ethiopian noblewomen. Today the finest ladies' dresses, *shammas*, and trousers are made of the 'country fabric' to which Parkyns alluded. Weaving and embroidery – in a variety of synthetic fabrics as well as silk – is exclusively executed by men. However, contemporary garments echo many of the features of nineteenth-century female attire. Dresses and trousers are frequently embroidered around the neck, cuffs, hem or ankles. The embroidered frontal panels, often culminating in a variety of motifs based on the cross, reflect regional variations, as does the cut of the dress. In some areas the shirt-like, waistless style of the nineteenth century is worn, whereas in Addis Ababa and other large cities a tailored style, with high waist and flared skirt, has developed.

Cloth of Church and State

The orthodox Christian church of Ethiopia acted as both customer and protector for a variety of craftspeople who produced a rich array of vestments, altar-cloths, wall-hangings and a host of other textile-based artefacts for ecclesiastical use.

Among the most intriguing of these artefacts are the heavy silk hanging panels, one example of which is in the British Museum, the other, in triptych form, being in the collections of the Royal Ontario Museum in Canada. According to two scholars (Gervers and Balicka-Witakowska, forthcoming), the hangings are the largest known examples of tablet weaving in the world (each panel requiring well in excess of three hundred tablets, through each one of which four warp threads would have passed), and were almost certainly woven in Gondar in the late eighteenth century using thick, locally spun yarn made from raw Chinese silk which is known to have been imported at this time. It has been further suggested by the same scholars that the two central figures on both the British Museum and Royal Ontario examples represent Queen Mentaub and her son Iyasu walking in procession together with retainers, clerics and armed men. Evidence of a range of associated, though less elaborate, textiles is provided by another large, tablet-woven silk cloth in the collections of the British Museum which was almost certainly woven at a similar time to the hanging described above, and quite possibly by the same

LEFT Panel of tablet-woven silk, the central element of a triptych, probably woven in Gondar during the late eighteenth century and designed to hang in a church. It apparently depicts a procession of royal, ecclesiastical and military figures, including Queen Mentaub (top) and her son Iyasu (immediately below). L:306 cm; w:63 cm. 1868,10–1.22.

RIGHT Woman's dress (*kamis*) of cotton, with rayon and lurex embroidery. This modern dress, made in 1993, is of a type worn by well-to-do women on special occasions in Addis Ababa and other cities of the central and northern highlands of Ethiopia. Both the weaving of the fine cotton base cloth and the embroidery are executed by male craftsmen. The dress has developed from a garment worn and elaborately embroidered by nineteenth-century Ethiopian noblewomen. L:140 cm; w:117 cm. 1993,Af16.1a.

ABOVE A noblewoman of Tegré and her servant in the mid-nineteenth century. The noblewoman is wearing a *shamma* with red border and a cotton tunic richly embroidered with silk thread. Skilful embroidery was a fashionable accomplishment and pastime amongst Ethiopian noblewomen of this period. Today, women's garments of a similar type are embroidered by men. From T. Lefebvre, *Voyage en Abyssinie*, Paris 1845–8.

guild of weavers. It has a series of loops along one edge through which a bar must have passed which suggests that it was hung horizontally rather than vertically, perhaps as an altar-cloth. There are no naturalistic representations in the patterning of the cloth, but the colour and thickness of the raw silk yarn, and the distinctive technique employed, are otherwise virtually identical to those of the hanging.

The technique of tablet weaving is by no means unknown in Africa, but other

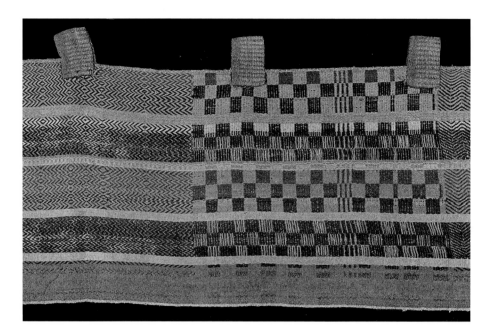

Detail of a tablet-woven silk hanging, probably made in late eighteenth-century Gondar for use in a church. A rod must have been passed through the loops along the upper edge of the textile. L:496 cm; w:68 cm. 1973,Af38.1.

examples of cloth made through this complex process are confined to small, but hard-wearing, items such as the belts, girdles and sashes of Morocco and Algeria. Furthermore, we know of no other examples of tablet-woven cloth from Ethiopia. However, tablet weaving is a craft practised by Jewish weavers in Morocco and in Yemen (Klein 1979:425–45). There was also a renowned group of Falasha weavers working in the Gondar/Lake Tana area producing other types of cloth (Pankhurst 1964:224), so it is not unreasonable to speculate that a specialist guild of Jewish tablet weavers existed in Gondar to produce these textiles.

Groups of craftsmen of Armenian origin seem to have been responsible for much of the fine embellishment in silver and other precious metals which characterised the robes worn by royalty, nobility and high-ranking officials of both church and state (Zeleke, personal correspondence). The imported velvet and silk cloth which forms the basis of many of these robes became more widely available during the nineteenth century, due in part to increased trading networks following the gradual unification of the empire. Another factor was the availability, from the beginning of the eighteenth century, of the Maria Theresa dollar, a coin minted in vast quantities in Austria and widely used in trade with north and north-east Africa. Until then, silver had been very difficult to obtain in Ethiopia. When melted down, these coins provided the raw material for the wonderful silver filigree work which adorns the finest robes.

Perhaps the most distinctive of these rich garments were the capes (*lamd*) worn by Ethiopian clerics, nobles and high-ranking military and secular officials, particularly during the late nineteenth and early twentieth centuries. The basic form of the garment is of a broad section which fits over the shoulders, from which hang as many as seven ornate, pendent panels, the extremities of which are often tailored into arabesque shapes. Each cape is richly embroidered with a combination of coloured thread, metal braid and glass, though the differences in design are probably indicative of the owner's individual taste and the dictates of fashion rather than of particular rank or status. The cape of a *dejazmach* or governor of a province is, however, somewhat different, having a higher collar and fewer and less ornate pendent panels, though the embroidery in gold braid is far finer and more detailed. It seems likely that these garments represent, in stylised form, the lion skin honorific capes which were traditionally worn by the nobility, the pendent panels with their decorative tips imitating the legs and paws of the lion.

Country Cloth: the Konso and Dorze of Southern Ethiopia

Much of the finest cloth in Ethiopia is today produced by two peoples who live close to one another in the southern highlands: the Konso and Dorze. Yet the weaving tradition in this part of the country is of comparatively recent origin compared with the central and northern highlands. Konso oral tradition has it that weaving was brought to the region by immigrant craftsmen, before which the people clothed themselves with animal skins. This may be one reason why weavers, along with other craftsmen also thought to be of immigrant origin such as blacksmiths and potters, are regarded as a separate class by other Konso, and are excluded from institutions such as the age-grading system which are fundamental to Konso culture. Another reason for this discrimination may be that weavers work with a substance, cotton, which has long been reviled by the Konso, not only because it ripens in the dry season and is therefore associated with drought and its attendant privations, but also because the colour white, the colour of bleached bones, is closely connected with death in the Konso symbolic code (Hallpike 1972:143,280). The repellent qualities of both raw cotton and bone are powerful prophylactics against the evil eye, a single cotton thread surrounding a Konso homestead being deemed sufficient to perform this function. However, though the weaver's raw material and its colour may be taboo in Konso society, the strong white cloth into which it is made finds a ready local market. Relatively little is traded outside the remote and insular lands of the Konso, however, and Konso weavers, unlike their counterparts among the neighbouring Dorze people, rarely migrate to the large towns in search of other outlets for their products.

We have shown how Dorze weavers from the Gamu highlands produce both the cotton cloth and the patterned silk border for the finest *shammas* worn in many parts of Ethiopia. However, in common with weavers among the Konso, Sidama and other peoples of the region, they also produce garments which have a particular social and ritual significance which is peculiar to this part of the country. The most notable of such garments are the brightly coloured, loose fitting sleeveless smocks and, in particular, the trousers of the same material which are known as *dunguse* among the Dorze, *gonfa* among the Sidama, and *bariti* among the Konso (Karsten 1972:91–2). The trousers are simply tailored by sewing together four rectangular pieces of cloth to make the legs, and two smaller, square pieces to form the gusset. Formerly, the *dunguse* trousers were reserved for wear only on certain occasions and by particular people among the

Two silk-lined velvet panels, embroidered with gold braid and sequins. L:36 cm; w:39 cm (top). 1974,Af11.7b. L:29 cm; w:29 cm. 1974,Af11.6a.

Two noblemen's capes (*lamd*) of silk-lined velvet embroidered with gold thread and with floral patterns in silk, embellished with brass and coloured glass. The cape on the right could be worn only by a *dejazmach* or governor of a province. Both garments, with their long, pendent sections, represent in stylised form the lion's skin capes traditionally worn by high-ranking secular and military officials. L:109 cm; w:103 cm. (left) 1974,Af11.12, L:113 cm; w:110 cm. 1974,Af11.11.

RIGHT Man's sleeveless top and trousers (*dunguse*) typical of those worn today on special occasions by Dorze men of the Gamu Gofa highlands of southern Ethiopia and, in a similar style, by the neighbouring Konso and Sidama peoples. Formerly the use of such costumes was much more restricted. The colours black (signifying rain) and red (signifying blood and meat) are very propitious. Yellow and white, by contrast, symbolise death. L:66 cm; w:55 cm. (top) 1993,Af16.6a&b. L:98 cm; w:62 cm.

Dorze such as the *halakas* or elders of the community, warriors who had slain an enemy in battle, and newly circumcised youths on their first appearance in public (Schaedler 1987:418). Today they are much more widely worn, particularly on the occasion of the Masqal festival of late September which celebrates the bringing of fragments of the True Cross to Ethiopia from the Holy Land during the fourteenth century (Olmstead 1973:131).

These smocks and trousers were traditionally patterned with weft stripes, predominantly of black and red, divided by much narrower stripes of pale yellow, though today machine-spun, aniline-dyed yarn is more available to the weavers, who produce the garments in different colours. The traditional black, yellow and red are still, however, the favoured combination. It has been suggested (Karsten 1972:92) that the reason for the abiding popularity of these colours is that before aniline mill yarn became available, local weavers had to trade with a neighbouring people who could produce naturally dyed yarn in these three colours only. A more likely explanation, or at least another factor to be considered, lies in the probable symbolic significance of these colours. Among the Konso, black is associated with the colour of rain clouds which bring an end to the dry season and life to the land and its inhabitants (Hallpike 1972:281); red is the colour of meat, another source of life, though it can also be interpreted as the blood of a warrior shed in battle. Both red and black are, therefore, highly propitious. The only other colour of deep significance to the Konso is white, which, as we have already shown, symbolises death. It may be that the narrow bands of pale yellow which separate the larger areas of red and black on the ceremonial garments have the value of white in this context. Indeed, the Konso word for yellow, *pudiyada*, has as its root the word for white, *aada*. Whether these colours are as important to other peoples of the region as they are to the Konso has not yet been demonstrated. What seems certain is that the colours have a particular significance when used on these garments which goes far beyond the visual impact which they make as a pleasing, decorative combination.

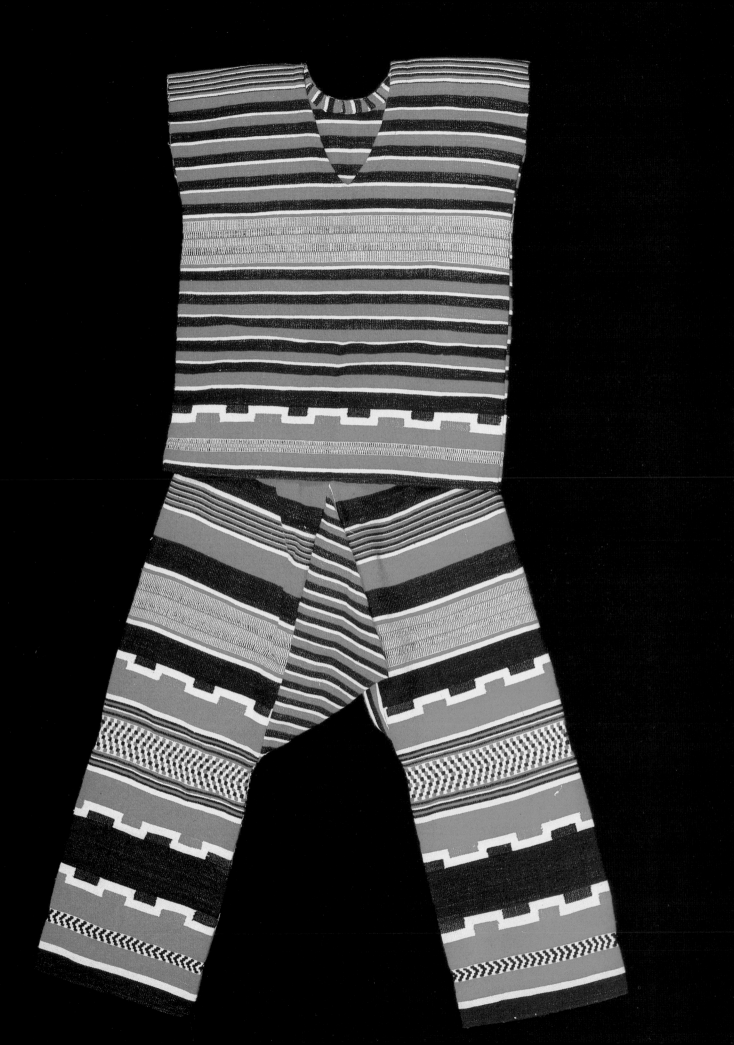

8

CONTINUITY AND CHANGE

This book attempts to give an insight into the cultural significance of North African textiles, both historically and in a contemporary context. However, such an overview must inevitably be qualified by the relative lack of knowledge of the historical processes which have shaped the tradition, and the undeniable rapidity of the social, economic and technological changes which are taking place, not just within the region, but throughout Africa. Perhaps the only certain thing which can be said about the North African textile tradition today is that it will not be the same tomorrow and will have adapted itself in a number of ways to accommodate changing tastes, materials and markets. However, this is to be expected of a dynamic phenomenon, and challenges the widespread assumption that the production of handmade textiles in Africa will cease, or at least be irretrievably debased, in the face of new technology, the wholesale importation of foreign textiles, and the gradual disintegration of the political, social and religious structures of non-industrialised societies. The various cultural forces inherent in a tradition will not vanish, simply because the social stimuli and technologies which carry that tradition forward are changing. The loom, even in its simplest form, is a machine and, therefore, it would be foolish totally to exclude factory-made cloth from the so-called 'handmade' textile tradition.

Many misconceptions about African art are based on the belief that, whatever its form, it will inevitably be tainted by any association with commercialism, which is often seen to be the primary cause of a perceived decline in

Detail of the back of a late nineteenth-century man's silk robe ('*aba*') a garment which at that time was woven and tailored in a similar style in several parts of the Arab world, notably in the town of Damascus, Syria. This example was woven in Egypt, quite possibly in the old silk weaving town of Naqada. L:135 cm; w:130 cm. 1994,Af3.1.

standards of workmanship. Although certain types of North African textile have been made purely for domestic consumption, fine quality cloths have always been traded, both within the continent and overseas. The eleventh-century grave goods found at Bandiagara, Mali, include the earliest examples of textiles found in sub-Saharan Africa, though a number are clearly of North African manufacture, indicating the existence of well-established, long-distance trading networks. During the sixteenth century, vast numbers of North African cloths were traded to the West African coast, the Portuguese

Tapestry-woven cloth, inspired by ancient 'Coptic' textiles, of a type which began to be made by children in the early 1950s at the Ramses Wissa Wassef workshop in Harraniya, a village to the north of Cairo. L:95 cm; w:137 cm (author's collection).

OPPOSITE, LEFT AND RIGHT A silk and cotton, tapestry-woven modesty garment (left) of the type once commonly worn by women of Bahriya Oasis, and a recently woven rayon version of the same design. Both cloths were woven in Upper Egypt at the town of Naqada in the Nile valley. L:235 cm; w:138 cm (left). 1991,Af11.7. L:424 cm; w:77 cm. 1993,Af24.7.

OPPOSITE, BELOW Woman from the town of Naqada in Upper Egypt weaving a rayon cloth on a small, treadle loom. Until the mid-twentieth century, cloths of this design, in subdued colours, were woven in silk and cotton for use as a modesty garment, particularly among women of Bahriya Oasis in Egypt's Western Desert. More recently, these bright, rayon versions found a market in Libya and Sudan. Today, trade with these 'traditional' markets has dwindled, and the weavers of Naqada are looking to foreign visitors and overseas markets as outlets for their skilfully woven cloths.
Photo: J. Mellors.

entreneurs feeding an existing predilection for Berber textiles in this region, which previously had been satisfied only by the relatively small numbers of cloths carried by the trans-Saharan caravans. Interestingly enough, even then there were complaints about declining standards of workmanship caused by over-production (Vogt 1975:636).

As elsewhere in the continent, the commercial weavers of North Africa have adapted themselves rapidly to new, sometimes synthetic, materials and to changing markets. Kerdassa, a small town not far from Cairo, once supplied cloth to Chad, Libya, Sudan and Tunisia, as well as to the oases of the Western Desert. In recent years these markets have largely dried up, though male weavers have adapted themselves and their looms to make commercial products such as versalia, a fabric used in the lining of hand luggage and clothing. They also make tapestry-woven cloth, *goblan*, inspired by so-called 'Coptic' textiles, for sale mainly to tourists. This 'line' was pioneered by the hugely popular children's tapestries made at the Ramses Wissa Wassef workshop in Harraniya, a village to the north of Cairo, in the early 1950s, and has since spawned a thousand imitators throughout Egypt. Women in Kerdassa tailor a wide variety of garments for local use, and also exploit the tourist trade where possible, as in the recent 'craze' for a type of *gallabiya* embroidered in the style of Siwa oasis (Lynch and Fahmy 1984:26–9).

Another popular product among male, treadle-loom weavers in Kerdassa

and other Egyptian towns, are rag-work textiles, the charming feature of which is their discontinuous weft created from numerous off-cuts of machine-made cloth and other materials such as plastic bags. Every element is wound onto its own separate bobbin, each one of which is fitted into a large shuttle boat and passed carefully through the shed for perhaps two or three picks, depending on the thickness of the off-cut. Such material is by no means distinctively Egyptian, or even North African, being woven in many parts of the world. However, it is worth mentioning here as a good example of a technique which thrives off the mechanised weaving industry, yet cannot easily be imitated by it. The resulting material has a wide range of uses, and may be bought by local people as much as by tourists. It is more robust than conventional textiles, and is currently very popular in Egypt for covering car seats.

A similar response to diminishing or changing markets may be observed in the town of Naqada in Upper Egypt, which for many centuries has provided fine tapestry-woven cloth from which were made garments such as the man's sleeveless silk robe, 'aba' and the modesty garment, in subdued colours of maroon and black silk and cotton, worn by married women of the oases of the Western desert, particularly Bahriya. When demand for the latter garment began to wane in the mid-twentieth century, the weavers of Naqada used essentially the same pattern, but wove the garment from bright, shiny, rayon yarn in many colours, which was more to the taste of the Sudanese and Libyan women who now bought it and wore it as a conventional wrap or shawl. More recently still, these new markets have become inaccessible because of political tension, and with the tourist market diminished in Egypt itself for similar reasons, the weavers of Naqada suffered extreme economic hardship. In response to this crisis an assisted silk weaving project was initiated. In the context of the division of labours in the weaving tradition throughout North Africa, one of the innovative features of this scheme is that many of the weavers are women. Until recently, the use of a treadle loom by a woman anywhere in Africa was unheard of, and certainly in Egypt was strictly taboo (Lynch and Fahmy 1984:26). However, a relaxation of the male domination of treadle-loom weaving was noted in Tunisia as long ago as the late 1960s (Teitelbaum 1976:73), and has also been documented elsewhere in Africa, for example in south-eastern Nigeria (Aronson 1982). The involvement of women in commercial weaving, but using looms conventionally associated with their sex, is a much older phenomenon in North Africa, particularly in the Maghrib countries, where it was initially encouraged by the colonial authorities. This tendency towards change in the conventional, gender-orientated division of labours seems likely to continue, not only in the weaving tradition but in a range of other activities. Whether such changes may be viewed as steps towards the emancipation of women in the region, or simply manifestations of a general process of capitalist transformation, is a debatable point.

In Ethiopia, male treadle-loom weavers from rural areas, such as Dorze from the southern highlands, have tended to gravitate towards the larger towns, for part of the year at least. There they might form a co-operative, perhaps with a middleman to sell their wares, or sell directly from the premises. Skilful weavers of the *tibeb*, the multicoloured, patterned border of the *shamma*, today provide their customers with an innovative range of colours and designs, including figurative motifs, to suit every taste. Some of the income they earn from weaving might be used to employ men to work their farms in their

A modern, sleeveless summer dress (*kamis*) and shawl (*natala*) from Ethiopia. L:124 cm; w:70 cm (dress). 1993,Af16.3a. L:234 cm; w:160 cm. 1993,Af16.3b.

homeland (Olmstead 1973:135). The cloth they weave in this urban environment is now no longer used exclusively for clothing, but might be made up into curtains, bed covers, table cloths and a range of other household items. Similarly, the style of embroidery once practised by noblewomen for the embellishment of their dresses, is today largely men's work, and the dresses themselves, sometimes styled to suit modern tastes, are worn by a far greater number of women in Ethiopian society.

Karsten (1972:120) noted an increasing demand for milled cloth in the southern highlands of Ethiopia, but commented that this was not having a particularly damaging effect on the remaining hand-loom weavers because it was simply part of an increasing demand for woven cloth (as opposed to leather or skins) in these remote rural areas. Furthermore, the coloured smocks and trousers characteristic of the Dorze and neighbouring Sidama and Konso peoples are now being much more generally worn (Schaedler 1987:418) than was formerly permitted, thus providing another source of income for the hand-loom weaver. This relaxation of the strict dress code once reserved exclusively to only a few members of society may be observed in other parts of Africa. The wearing of *kente* cloth among the Asante of Ghana, for example, was once the

Modern, woollen textile from Oued Zem in central Morocco. Woven by a Berber woman, probably using a metal-framed, upright loom, the cloth is covered with representational images of men, women and various animals. The weaver has playfully taken her revenge on some of the male shepherds depicted on the cloth by removing their heads. In common with many other modern Berber textiles, this cloth has been artificially aged with sulphur in order to make the bright colours of the wool more subdued, and therefore supposedly more attractive to the Western taste. One corner has been missed, however. L:170 cm; w:98 cm. 1994,Af2.1.

prerogative of royalty and a select group of chiefs, whereas today it has become accepted formal attire amongst well-to-do Ghanaians – not to mention people of the African diaspora around the world – in place of, or in combination with, a suit and tie. Similarly, the Ethiopian *shamma* may today be worn by both men and women in combination with Western dress.

This concluding section of the book has so far largely considered the situation of those who have always produced handmade cloth for commercial purposes in North Africa. However, a large proportion of textiles, historically at least, was produced solely for domestic consumption, or occasionally for exchange within a ceremonial or ritual context. Such textiles were mainly produced by women, either on the ground loom or, in the Maghrib, on the upright, single-heddle Berber loom. The products of the ground loom, particularly tent cloths, are no longer in such demand, largely because of the gradual transformation of the life-style of many of the indigenous peoples of the region from a nomadic or transhumant to a more sedentary pattern. The decorative textiles produced on the Berber loom, by contrast, continue to be woven in large quantities, though nowadays as often as not in an urban environment, for non-Berber clients and for commercial purposes. They may also be woven on a metal loom which, although of exactly the same construction as the wooden, collapsible Berber loom, produces a noticeably more regular weave because of its rigid structure. Aniline dyes and machine-spun or synthetic yarns are frequently used, though, as Forelli and Harries (1977:47) pointed out almost twenty years ago, the use of milled cotton to produce white patterns in certain types of cloth produced in Azrou (Morocco) was already considered 'traditional'.

In some ways the changes affecting women's weaving in the Maghrib are similar to developments in West Africa, where women traditionally wove cloth on an upright loom for domestic and utilitarian use. Today, however, women in West Africa often weave different types of textile for a different clientele. For example, in recent years the female weavers of Akwete in south-eastern Nigeria organised themselves into a co-operative in order to manufacture and to expand the market for their product more effectively, both within Nigeria and abroad (Aronson 1991).

During the French colonial period in North Africa, the goverment-sponsored 'artisanat' movement sought to record and preserve the weaving tradition, together with the other indigenous crafts of the region. One means of achieving this aim was to encourage weavers to produce a regulated, standardised and commercially viable product which would help them to resist competition from other sources and thus perpetuate the tradition. In some ways the 'artisanat' movement could be said to have achieved its aim, in that Berber weaving continues to thrive today, under the regulatory eye of similar government institutions of the post-colonial era. However, this attempt to 'fix the language' of a tradition which formerly had no commercial basis inevitably led to the loss of much of the significance surrounding the weaving of cloth, together with numerous associated customs and rituals referred to by Messick (1987:210–25) as the 'subordinate discourse' of women. Whether a new, adapted type of discourse will emerge remains to be seen. The long history and dynamism of the textile tradition in North Africa suggests, perhaps, that it will.

BIBLIOGRAPHY

ABU ZAHRA, N., 1982, *Sidi Ameur – a Tunisian Village*, London.

ABU-LUGHOD, L., 1986, *Veiled Sentiments. Honor and Poetry in a Bedouin Society*, Berkeley and Los Angeles.

ABUN-NASR, J. M., 1975, (2nd edn), *A History of the Maghrib*, Cambridge.

ABDELKAFI, 1977, *Weddings in Tripolitania*, Tripoli.

ADAM, A., 1952, 'Le costume dans quelques tribus de l'Anti-Atlas', *Hespéris*, XXXIX:459–85.

AMMAR, H., 1954, *Growing up in an Egyptian Village*, London.

AMMOUN, D., 1991, *Crafts of Egypt*, Cairo.

ANTOUN, R. A., 1968, 'On the Modesty of Women in Arab Muslim Villages: A Study in the Accommodation of Traditions', *American Anthropologist*, 70:671–97.

ARONSON, L., 1982, 'Popo weaving: the dynamics of trade in southeastern Nigeria', *African Arts*, vol. XV, 3:43–7.

ARONSON, L., 1991, 'African women in the visual arts', *Signs: Journal of Women in Culture and Society*, vol. XVI, 3:549–74.

BAFFOUN, A., 1982, 'Women and Social Change in the Muslim Arab World', *Women's Studies International Forum*, vol. 5, 2:227–42.

BARCLAY, H. B., 1964, *Buurri al Lamaab: a Suburban Village in the Sudan*, New York.

BAYRAM, A., 1977, 'Rites de passage et initiation dans le mariage traditionnel tunisois', *Cahiers des Arts et Traditions Populaires*, 6:5–10.

BEN-AMI, A., 1989, 'Decorated Shrouds from Tétouan, Morocco', *The Israel Museum Journal*, vol. VIII, Spring:31–40.

BENFOUGHAL, T., 1983, *Les costumes féminins de Tunisie. Collection du Musée du Bardo d'Alger*, Algiers.

BENT, J. T. and BENT, M. V. A., 1900, *Southern Arabia*, London.

BERNÈS, J. P., 1974, *Maroc costumes, broderies, brocarts*, Paris.

BESANCENOT, J., 1990, *Costumes of Morocco*, London and New York.

BLACKMAN, W. S., 1927, *The Fellahin of Upper Egypt*, London.

BLISS, F., 1982, 'Das Kunsthandwerk der Oase Siwa (Ägypten)', *Baessler-Archiv, Neue Folge*, XXX:1–63.

BOURILLY, J. and LAOUST, E., 1927, *Stèles Funéraires Marocaines*, Paris.

BYNON, J., 1984, 'Berber Women's Pottery: is the decoration motivated?', in Picton, J. (ed.), *Earthenware in Asia and Africa*, London.

CALLENDAR, C. and EL GUINDI, F., 1971, 'Life-Crisis Rituals Among the Kenuz', *Case Western Reserve University Studies in Anthropology*, no. 3, Cleveland and London.

CARTER, H., 1933, *The tomb of Tut-ankh-amen*, vol. III, New York.

CHANTREAUX, G., 1944, 'Les tissages décorés chez les Beni-Mguild', *Hespéris*, XXXI: 19–45.

CHANTREAUX, G., 1946, 'Notes sur un procédé de tissage torsade', *Hespéris*, XXXIII:65–81.

CHENNELLS, E., 1893, *Recollections of an Egyptian princess by her English governess: being a record of five years' residence at the court of Ismael Pasha, Khédive*, vol. I, London.

CHURCHILL, W. S., 1899, *The River War*, 2 vols, London.

CLOUDSLEY, A., 1983, *Women of Omdurman: life, love and the cult of virginity*, London.

COLLINGWOOD, P. D., 1982, *The Techniques of Tablet Weaving*, New York.

COMBES, J. and S., 1945, 'De la laine en suint aux files', *I.B.L.A.*, nos. 31–2.

CROWFOOT, G. M., 1921, 'Spinning and weaving in the Sudan', *Sudan Notes and Records*, vol. IV, 1:20–38.

CROWFOOT, G. M., 1924, 'The handspinning of cotton in the Sudan', *Sudan Notes and Records*, vol. VII, 2:83–9.

CROWFOOT, G. M. and DAVIES, de G. N., 1941, 'The tunic of Tutankhamun', *The Journal of Egyptian Archaeology* 27:112–30.

CROWFOOT, J. W., 1922, 'Wedding Customs in the Northern Sudan', *Sudan Notes and Records*, vol. V, 1:1–28.

CROWFOOT, J. W., 1932, 'Popular Rites in the Northern Sudan: their place and significance', in *Studies Presented to F. Ll. Griffith*, London.

DESTA, S., 1957, 'Cottage Crafts: Spinning and Weaving', *Ethiopia Observer*, vol. 1, 3:90–1.

DODDS, J. D., ed., 1992, *Al-Andalus – The Art of Islamic Spain*, New York.

DONNE, J. B., 1981, 'Tripod Looms', *Hali*, vol. 4, 2:147–50.

DONOVAN, N., 1973, 'Tsion Andom of Ethiopia', *African Arts*, vol. VIII, 1:38–9.

DOZY, R. P. A., 1845, *Dictionnaire Détaillé des Noms des Vêtements chez les Arabes*, Amsterdam.

EL-MESSIRI, S., 1978, *Ibn al-Balad: A Concept of Egyptian Identity*, in Social, Economic and Political Studies of the Middle East, No. 24, Leiden.

FAKHOURI, H., 1972, *Kafr el-Elow. An Egyptian Village in Transition*, New York.

FAKHRY, A., 1973, *The Oases of Egypt: Siwa Oasis*, vol. I, Cairo.

FAKHRY, A., 1974, *The Oases of Egypt: Bahriyah and Farafra Oases*, vol. II, Cairo.

FEENY, J., 1986, 'Tentmakers of Cairo', *Aramco World Magazine*, vol. 37, 6:16–25.

FERNEA, R. A. and GERSTER, G., 1973, *Nubians in Egypt, Peaceful People*, Austin.

FERNEA, R. A. and E. W., 1991, *Nubian Ethnographies*, Illinois.

FORELLI, S. and HARRIES, J., 1977, 'Traditional Berber Weaving in Central Morocco', *The Textile Museum Journal*, vol. 4, 4:41–60.

FORELLI, S. and HARRIES, J., 1980, 'Domestic Weaving in Central Morocco: Three Contemporary Examples', in Fiske, P. L. et al. (eds), *From the Far West: Carpets and Textiles of Morocco*, Washington, D.C.

FOX, G. L., 1977, '"Nice Girl": Social Control of Women through a Value Construct', *Signs: Journal of Women in Culture and Society*, vol. 2, 4:805–17.

GALLOTTI, J., 1939, 'Weaving and Dyeing in North Africa', *CIBA Review*, 21:734–64.

GARGOURI-SETHOM, S., 1986, *Le Bijou Traditionnel en Tunisie: femmes parées, femmes enchaînées*, Aix-en-Provence.

GEERTZ, C., GEERTZ, H. and ROSEN, L., 1979, *Meaning and order in Moroccan society. Three essays in cultural analysis*, Cambridge.

GERVERS, M., and BALICKA-WITAKOWSKA, E., (forthcoming), 'Two Ethiopian card-woven silk curtains', *Proceedings of the Third International Conference on Ethiopian Art*, Addis Ababa, November 1993.

GLEICHEN, A. E. W., 1905, *The Anglo-Egyptian Sudan*, 2 vols, London.

GILFOY, P. S., 1987, *Patterns of Life: West African Strip-Weaving Traditions*, Washington D.C. and London.

GILFOY, P. S., 1992, 'The Eye, the Hand and the Stripe: North African Designs in West African Strip-Woven Textiles', in *History, Design and Craft in West-African Strip-Woven Cloth*, Washington, D.C.

GODLEY, A. D., 1926, *Herodotus*, vol. I, Books I & II, London.

GOICHON, A-M., 1927, *La vie féminine au Mzab: étude de sociologie musulmane*, Paris.

GOLDBERG, H. E., 1980, *The Book of Mordechai: A Study of the Jews of Libya*, Philadelphia.

GOLOMBEK, L., 1988, 'The Draped Universe of Islam', in Soucek, P. P. (ed.), *Content and context of visual arts in the Islamic World*, London.

GOLVIN, L., 1950, 'Le "métier à la tire." Des Fabricants de Brocarts de Fès', *Hespéris*, XXXVII:21–52.

GROHMANN, A., 1934, 'Tiraz', *Encyclopaedia of Islam*, IV: 785–93.

HALL, M. and ISMAIL, B. A., 1981, *Sisters under the Sun: The Story of Sudanese Women*, London and New York.

HALLPIKE, C. R., 1972, *The Konso of Ethiopia*, Oxford.

HARRIES, J., 1973, 'Pattern and choice in Berber weaving and poetry', *Research in African Literatures*, vol. 4, 2:141–53.

HARRIES, J. and RAAMOUCH, M., 1971, 'Berber popular songs of the Middle Atlas', *African Language studies*, 12:52–70.

HARRIS, J. (ed.), 1993, *5,000 Years of Textiles*, London.

HEATHCOTE, D., 1972, 'Insight into a creative process: a rare collection of embroidery drawings from Kano', *Savanna*, vol. I, 2:165–74.

HEATHCOTE, D., 1973, 'Hausa women's dress in the light of two recent finds', *Savanna*, vol. II, 2:201–17.

HEATHCOTE, D., 1976, 'Hausa Embroidered Dress', *African Arts*, vol. V, 2:12–19.

HEFFENING, W., 1934, '"urs', *The Encyclopaedia of Islam*, IV:1038–47.

HOLT, P. M., 1958, *The Mahdist State in the Sudan*, Oxford.

HUNT, C., 1980, 'Berber Brides' Fair', *The National Geographic Magazine*, vol. 157, 1:118–29.

IMPERATO, P. J., 1973, 'Wool Blankets of the Peul of Mali', *African Arts*, vol. VII, 3:40–7.

IMPERATO, P. J., 1976, 'Kereka Blankets of the Peul', *African Arts*, vol. IX, 4:56–9.

IMPERATO, P. J., 1979, 'Blankets and Covers from the Niger Bend', *African Arts*, vol. XII, 4:38–43.

JOHNSTON, C., 1844, *Travels in Southern Abyssinia*, 2 vols, London.

JOUIN, J., 1931, 'Iconographie de la mariée citadine dans l'Islam Nord-Africain', *Revue des Études Islamiques*, 5:313–39.

JOUIN, J., 1936, 'Le costume de la femme Israélite au Maroc', *Journal de la Société des Africanistes*, VI:167–85.

KARSTEN, D., 1972, *The Economics of Handicrafts in Traditional Societies*, Munich.

KENNEDY, J. G. (ed.), 1978, *Nubian Ceremonial Life*, Los Angeles.

KENYON, S. (ed.), 1987, *The Sudanese Woman*, Oxford.

KLEIN, A., 1979, 'Tablet Weaving by the Jews of San'a (Yemen)', in Cordwell, J. M. and Schwartz, R. A. (eds), *The Fabrics of Culture*, The Hague, Paris and New York.

KNIGHT, I., 1986, 'Mahdist Jibbehs', *Miniature War Games*, vol. 43, December: 30–5.

LANE, E. W., 1871, *An Account of the Manners and Customs of the Modern Egyptians*, 2 vols, London.

LAPANNE-JOINVILLE, J., 1940, 'Les Métiers à Tisser de Fes', *Hespéris*, XXVII:21–65.

LEFEBVRE, T., 1845–8, *Voyage en Abyssinie*, 3 vols, Paris.

LEOPOLDO, B., 1986, *The Oasis of Amun-Siwa*, Geneva.

LEVTZION, N. and HOPKINS, J. F. P. (eds), 1981, *Corpus of early arabic sources for West African history*, Cambridge.

LOUIS, A., 1979, *Nomades d'hier et d'aujourd'hui dans le sud Tunisien*, Aix-en-Provence.

LYNCH, P. D. and FAHMY, H., 1984, *Crafts women in Kerdassa, Egypt*, Geneva.

MACLEOD, A. E., 1991, *Accommodating Protest: Working Women, the New Veiling, and Change in Cairo*, New York.

MARCAIS, P., 1979, '"ayn', *Encyclopaedia of Islam*, vol 1:785–6.

MEHREZ, S., 1993, *Women's Costumes in the Egyptian Countryside, Oases and Deserts*, Cairo.

MESSICK, B., 1987, 'Subordinate discourse: women, weaving and gender relations in North Africa', *American Ethnologist*, vol. 14, 2:210–25.

MESSING, S. D., 1960, 'The Nonverbal Language of the Ethiopian Toga', *Anthropos*, vol. 55, no. 3–4:558–60.

MICAUD, E., 1970, 'The Craft Tradition in North Africa', *African Arts*, vol. III, 2:38–43.

MORIN-BARDE, M., 1990, *Coiffeures féminines du Maroc*, Aix-en-Provence.

MURRAY, G. W., 1935, *Sons of Ishmael: a Study of the Egyptian Bedouin*, London.

MULLER-LANCET, A., 1976, 'Elements in Costume and Jewellery Specific to the Jews of Morocco', *The Israel Museum News*, no. 11:46–66.

MULLER-LANCET, A. and CHAMPAULT, D. (eds.), 1986, *La Vie juive au Maroc*, Jerusalem and Tel Aviv.

OLIVER, R. and CROWDER, M. (eds), 1981, *The Cambridge Encyclopaedia of Africa*, Cambridge.

OLMSTEAD, J., 1973, 'Ethiopia's Artful Weavers', *National Geographic Magazine*, vol. 143, 1:125–41.

OUGOUAG-KEZZAL, C., 1970, 'Le costume et la parure de la mariée à Tlemcen', *Libyca*, XVIII:253–67.

PAINE, S., 1990, *Embroidered Textiles: Traditional Patterns from Five Continents*, London.

PANKHURST, R., 1964, 'The Old-time Handicrafts of Ethioipia', *Ethiopia Observer*, vol. 8, 3:221–42.

PARIENTI, R., 1953, 'Les Tissages Mozabites', *Cahiers des Arts et Techniques de l'Afrique du Nord*, 3:49–57.

PARK, C. C., 1980, 'The Weaving of Rural Arab Groups in the Tennsift River Region of Morocco', in Fiske, P. L. et al. (eds), *From the Far West: Carpets and Textiles of Morocco*, Washington D.C.

PARKYNS, M., 1853, *Life in Abyssinia*, 2 vols, London.

PICTON, J. and MACK, J., 1989, (2nd edn), *African Textiles*, London.

POINSSOT, L. and Revault, J., 1957, *Tapis Tunisiens*, vol. IV, Paris.

REMINICK, R. A., 1976, 'The Evil Eye Belief among the Amhara', in Maloney, C. (ed.), *The Evil Eye*, New York.

RENON, A., 1944, *Le Mouton*, Collection 'Le Bled', series 2, no. 1, Tunis.

RESWICK, I., 1981, 'Traditional Textiles of Tunisia', *African Arts*, vol. XIV, 3:56–65.

RESWICK, I., 1985, *Traditional Textiles of Tunisia*, Los Angeles.

REVAULT, J., 1960, 'Broderies Tunisiennes', *Cahiers de Tunisie*, VIII:137–57.

RICARD, P., 1925, 'Le Batik Berbére', *Hespéris*, vol. V, 4:411–26.

ROUSSEAU, M. A., 1852, 'Voyage du Scheikh et-Tidjani dans la régence de Tunis', *Journal Asiatique*, series IV, XX:171,200.

RUBENS, A., 1973, *A History of Jewish Costume*, London.

RUGH, A. B., 1984, *Family in Contemporary Egypt*, Cairo.

RUGH, A. B., 1986, *Reveal and Conceal: Dress in Contemporary Egypt*, New York.

SCHAEDLER, K-F., 1987, *Weaving in Africa South of the Sahara*, Munich.

SCHNEIDER, J., 1987, 'The Anthropology of Cloth', *Annual review of Anthropology*, 16:409–48.

SCARCE, J., 1987, *Women's Costume of the Near and Middle East*, London and Sydney.

SEFRIOUI, A., 1980, 'The Moroccan Carpet' in Fiske, P. L. et al (eds), *From the Far West: Carpets and Textiles of Morocco*, Washington, D.C.

SERJEANT, R. B., 1948, 'Material for a History of Islamic Textiles up to the Mongol Conquest: Egyptian Textiles', *Ars Islamica*, XIII–XIV:88–113.

SERJEANT, R. B., 1951, 'Material for a History of Islamic Textiles up to the Mongol Conquest: The Maghreb', *Ars Islamica*, XV–XVI:41–54.

SETHOM, S., 1968, 'La confection du costume féminin d'Hammamet', *Cahiers des Arts et Traditions Populaires*, 1:101–111.

SETHOM, S., 1969, 'La tunique de mariage en Tunisie', *Cahiers des Arts et Traditions Populaires*, 3:5–20.

SETHOM, S., 1976, 'Relations inter-régionales et costumes traditionnels féminins dans la Presqu'île du Cap-Bon', *Cahiers des Arts et Traditions Populaires*, 6:101–7.

SETHOM, S. et al., 1976, *Signes et Symboles dans l'Art Populaire Tunisien*, Tunis.

SIJELMASSI, M., 1986, *Les Arts Traditionnels au Maroc*, Paris.

SKHIRI, F., 1969, 'Deux Couvertures de Testour', *Cahiers des Arts et Traditions Populaires*, 3:21–39.

SKHIRI, F., 1971, 'Les châles des Matmata', *Cahiers des Arts et Traditions Populaires*, 4:49–53.

SLANE, M. de (trans), 1862–8, *Prolégomènes historiques*, vol. II, Paris.

STANZER, W., 1991, *Berber. Tribal Carpets and Weavings from Morocco*, Graz.

STILLMAN, Y. K., 1986, 'Libas', *Encyclopaedia of Islam*, V:732–46.

STONE, C., 1985, *The Embroideries of North Africa*, London.

SUGIER, C., 1969, 'Le thème du lion dans les arts populaires tunisiens', *Cahiers des Arts et Traditions Populaires*, 3:67–84.

TANFOUS, A., 1971, 'Les ceintures de femmes en Tunisie', *Cahiers des Arts et Traditions Populaires*, 4:103–122.

TEITELBAUM, J. M., 1976, 'The Leer and the Loom – Social Controls on Handloom Weavers', in Maloney, C. (ed.), *The Evil Eye*, New York.

TRIMINGHAM, J. S., 1949, *Islam in the Sudan*, Oxford.

TRIMINGHAM, J. S., 1971, *The Sufi Orders in Islam*, Oxford.

van GENNEP, A., 1911, *Études d'Ethnographie Algérienne*, Paris.

van GENNEP, A., 1960, *The Rites of Passage*, Chicago.

VIVIAN, C., 1990, *Islands of the Blest: A Guide to the Oases and Western Desert of Egypt*, Cairo.

VIVIER, M-F., 1995, 'Les voiles et les châles', in Cuénot, J. (ed.), *Noces tisées, Noces brodées: parures et costumes féminins de Tunisie*, Paris.

VOGT, J., 1975, 'Notes on the Portuguese Cloth Trade in West Africa, 1480–1540', *International Journal of African Historical Studies*, vol. VIII, 4:623–51.

WEINER, A. and SCHNEIDER, B., 1991, *Cloth and Human Experience*, Washington and London.

WEIR, S., 1970, *Spinning and Weaving in Palestine*, London.

WEIR, S., 1989, *Palestinian Costume*, London.

WELLS, S. H., 1911, 'L'Industrie de Tissage en Égypte', *Égypte Contemporaine*, 2:52–73.

WESTERDIJK, P., 1988, *The African Throwing Knife*, Utrecht.

WESTERMARCK, E., 1914, *Marriage Ceremonies in Morocco*, London.

WEYLAND, P., 1993, *Inside the Third World Village*, London and New York.

WINGATE, F. R., 1968, (2nd edn), *Mahdism and the Egyptian Sudan*, London.

YEDDER, A. M., 1982, 'The oral literature associated with the traditional wedding ceremony at Ghadames', unpublished doctoral thesis, London University: SOAS.

ZAHAN, D., 1975, 'Colours and Body Painting in Black Africa', *Diogenes*, 90:100–19.

ZENKOVSKY, S., 1945, 'Marriage Customs in Omdurman', *Sudan Notes and Records*, vol. XXVI, 2:241–55.

ZOUARI, A., 1980, 'Le mariage traditionnel à Sfax', *Cahiers des Arts et Traditions Populaires*, 7:157–9.

GLOSSARY

'abā': man's short, sleeveless, outer coat.

'ajār: Tunisian woman's silk veil with opaque central section and elaborately decorated end panels.

'amma: public.

'arīs: bridegroom.

'ayn: 'eye', in this context the 'evil eye'.

aada: Konso (Ethiopia) word for white, also associated with death.

adire: 'that which is tied and dyed', indigo resist-dyeing technique used by the Yoruba in Nigeria.

akhnif: wool and goat hair semi-circular hooded cloak, characterised by an enormous orange-red 'eye' design, worn by men and boys in Morocco.

aljaravias: North African hooded cloak with half sleeves traded by the Portuguese in West Africa.

almarfad: red woollen head-cloth worn by married women in Ghadames Oasis, Libya.

alquicés: North African white woollen cloth traded by the Portuguese in West Africa.

anṣār: 'helpers', a name given to the men of Medina who granted refuge to the Prophet Muhammad after the Hegira.

asherah nahuak: white embroidered dress worn by women from Siwa Oasis, Egypt, on the third day after marriage.

aska takwas: 'eight knives' design embroidered onto Hausa (Northern Nigeria) men's robes.

al-badla al-sha'bīya: 'national dress', requisite 'uniform' of khaki trousers and shirt worn by some factory workers in Egypt.

bakhnuq: Tunisian wool and cotton head-shawl.

banīqa: Algerian woman's embroidered linen cap, used to wrap up wet hair after bathing.

baraka: blessing of God.

bariti: Konso (Ethiopia) name for brightly coloured loose trousers.

barmaqli: a Turkish-derived open-work stitch, using flat metal thread, seen on Tunisian tunics.

buluko: heavy cotton shawl, used by men and women in Ethiopia as a sleeping blanket or a shroud.

dār el-ṭirāz: workshop or factory within the palace precinct for the production of ṭirāz.

darāwīsh: members of a religious fraternity; 'poor men', religious mendicants of Kordofan and Darfur, Sudan.

derfudit: blue and white checked cotton shawl worn by married women in Siwa Oasis, Egypt.

dejazmach: governor of a province in Ethiopia.

dīwan al-majlis: 'office of the council', under the Fatimids the first central administrative office.

dunguse: Dorze (Ethiopia) name for brightly coloured loose trousers.

faltita: gathered skirts worn by women of the Mesguita, Morocco.

farmala: short waistcoat worn in Tunisia and Libya.

farrāsh: Egyptian middleman or agent who rents out appliqué tents.

fātiḥa: the first Sura of the Qur'an, recited during the wedding ceremony.

flij: woven strips forming the 'roof' of a Berber tent.

gallābīya: long, loose robe worn by men in Egypt.

gandūra: sleeveless woollen tunic worn by men.

girgar: Nubian over-garment with a deep ruffle. The modern knee-length version is made of semi-transparent material.

goblan: tapestry-woven cloth produced in Egypt. The name derives from the french 'Gobelin'.

gonfa: Sidama (Ethiopia) name for brightly coloured loose trousers.

hadana: in the northern Sudan, the occasion after marriage when the bride and groom sit together at sunrise and sunset, with the bride's veil stretched over their heads.

halakas: elders of the community among the Dorze of southern Ethiopia.

ḥammām: steam bath.

handīra: woman's woollen shawl from Morocco.

ḥanṭoz: a triangular pad covered in gold-embroidered silk handkerchiefs, used by married women in Morocco.

ḥigāb: derived from the Arabic verb *hajaba*, 'to hide from view, conceal', a woman's veil.

ḥizām: belt used by men and women.

ḥizāma: the ceremony of 'undoing the belt'.

'īd al-fiṭr: the Feast of breaking the Ramadan fast.

jallaba: hooded outer robe with long sleeves worn mainly in Morocco.

jarbīya: piece of cloth used in Algeria to cover the bride and groom on their wedding night.

jarjara: Arabic verb meaning to trail, drag or shuffle.

jibbat al-'ayn fil-'ayn: 'the tunic of the eye against the eye', the openwork, gold-decorated tunic, used at the *jilwa* ceremony in Nabeul, Tunisia.

jihād: 'holy war', military activity concerned with the expansion of Islam.

jilwa: ceremony at which the bride is displayed publicly to the assembled guests and unveiled.

jird: man's white woollen cloak (Egypt).

jirtiq: Sudanese ceremony at which the bride and groom are invested with ornaments proper to their married status.

jubba: a long-sleeved outer garment, often open at the front. In the Sudan the term refers to the tunic with appliqué sections worn by the *anṣār*, the supporters of the Mahdi.

jubba maṭrūza: gold-embroidered wool gauze dress from Hammamet, Tunisia, with a distinctive plait of passementerie.

kaasa: woollen blanket from Mali produced on the double-heddle loom.

kamis: Ethiopian woman's cotton dress.

katfiya: woollen shoulder-cloth from Tunisia, used to prevent oil from the hair staining clothing.

katif: decorated velvet plastron worn as part of the *kiswat al-kabira* costume by women in Mogador, Salé and Rabat, Morocco.

kente: narrow-strip, multi-coloured cloth from Ghana, characterised by its complex patterns.

kerka: narrow-strip wool and goat hair blanket, woven in Niger.

khamsa: the number five; in North Africa it is imbued with a magical and protective value.

khayma: tent.

khila' (pl.): robes of honour.

khiyamiya: Egyptian tentmaker.

kilim trabelsi: wall or floor covering produced by weavers of Libyan descent in south-west Tunisia.

kiswat al-kabīra: 'the great dress', the ceremonial velvet costume of Moroccan Jews.

kumbayz: jacket with short sleeves, part of the ceremonial costume from Morocco.

kutta: medium-weight cotton shawl used by men and women in Ethiopia as a sleeping blanket or a shroud.

lailat al-dukhla: 'the night of entering', the wedding night.

lailat al-ḥinnā': 'the henna night', at which the bride, and often the groom, in separate ceremonies have their hands and feet dyed with henna.

lamba: generic term for cloth in Madagascar.

lambens: Portuguese term for woollen cloths of a specific design produced in North Africa for the West African market.

lamd: cape worn by Ethiopian nobility, clerics, royalty and high-ranking officials.

limut: plain coloured border on a *shamma*.

māshiṭa: a woman employed to provide the bride's wedding costume and jewellery, and to organise the entertainment in Tunisian rural areas.

milāk: engagement party.

milāya: woman's rectangular outer wrap.

mu'allim: male instructor or master of a textile workshop.

mu'allima: female embroidery teacher.

muḥaggaba: 'those who are veiled', the name adopted by women in Egypt who wear full-length outfits and cover their hair.

muqaddam: 'placed in front', the immediate subordinate of the Amir in the armies of the Mahdist state.

muraqqa'a: 'that which is put together from several pieces', the name given to the patched tunic of the Sufi initiate.

al-muwaḥḥidūn: 'the professors of the Unity of God'; the Western term, the Almohads, is derived from the Arabic.

mwashma: tattooed.

naggafa: woman from whom marriage costumes are hired in urban Morocco.

natala: lightweight Ethiopian cotton shawl worn by men and women.

nazāfa: cleanliness, tidiness.

pudiyada: Konso (Ethiopia) word for yellow.

qafṭān: 'caftan', a long-sleeved outer garment worn by men and women.

qamajja: rectangular tunic worn in Tunisia, a gold-embroidered version is worn at marriage in Moknine.

qarmasis: striped silk or synthetic cloth, used at three significant events in Sudanese women's lives: marriage, birth and circumcision.

qurbāb: long piece of cloth used as a garment by Sudanese women.

rashrash: plaited tresses from Dakhla Oasis, Egypt.

ridā' al-ḥalīb: 'veil of milk', cloth provided by the groom's father for the mother of the bride in Libya.

ru'us mi'at: 'captains of hundreds', commanders of the smallest sub-divisions in the Mahdist army (Sudan).

safsarī: large white rectangular cloth used by rural Tunisian women.

shamma: Ethiopian cotton shawl worn by men and women.

shintiyān: loose billowing women's trousers derived from Turkish styles.

shuqqa: long white cloak worn by the Kenuz bride (Nubia).

sidar: sleeveless vest or waistcoat worn by men in Egypt.

ṣīwān: large tent or pavilion.

smatt: double saddlebags, Morocco.

ṣūf: wool.

sūq: market.

surādiq: large tent or pavilion.

ṭa'ām: food or wedding feast.

ta'jīra: decorated woollen head-shawl used by women in Tunisia.

tahzīm: ceremony of 'putting on the belt'.

takhlīla: large rectangular cloth used as woman's garment in rural Tunisia

tāl: flat metal thread.

tanshīfa: embroidered linen cloth used by Algerian women draped around the shoulders or covering the hair.

ṭaqīya: cotton skullcap.

ṭarḥa: long head-veil worn by women in Sudan and Egypt, also used by young Sudanese girls outside the home.

ṭarīqa: 'path', method of instruction, initiation and religious exercise.

telli: silver threads embroidered on a fine net-like material, used to decorate dresses in Egypt, now rarely seen.

tet: Ethiopian fine cotton yarn.

tha'bān: brown and white striped woollen trousers, knitted by men in the High Atlas region, Morocco.

thawb: long cloth of plain or printed material worn by Sudanese women as a draped garment.

tibeb: multi-coloured patterned band of silk or rayon on a *shamma* (Ethiopia).

tihuna: diamond pattern used on houses and textiles, meaning 'small space', possibly providing protection for the owners.

ṭirāz: a term derived from the Persian, meaning 'embroidery'; it later came to be associated with robes decorated with bands of embroidered inscription; finally it denoted the workshop in which these textiles were produced.

ṭirāz al-'amm: public textile workshops.

'uqūs: plaited tresses used in Bahriya Oasis, Egypt.

waddah: presentation and display of engagement gifts among the Kenuz, Nubia.

yawm al-dukhla: the wedding day.

zaltita: a wrap-around skirt forming part of the Jewish ceremonial costume, the *kiswat al-kabira*.

ziyy islāmī: 'Islamic dress', long, concealing clothing and close-fitting headwear.

INDEX

'aba' 93, 136, *133*
Abbasids 19
Addis Ababa 120-1, 125, *125, 126*
adire 125
Agadir 24, 25
'ajar 31, 56, *95*
akhnif 90
Aksum 119-20, *39, 120, 121*
Algeria 13, 16-17, 24, 41, 55, 109, 128, *37, 41, 43, 69, 83, 84, 87, 97*
Algiers 17, 111, *93*
aljaravias 24
Almohads 16, 20, 21
Almoravids 16, 21
altar-cloth 31, 125, 128
Amhara 121
amulet 27, 53, 101, 103, 117, *104*
Andalusian 16, 21, 53, 56, 92, 93, 96, 111, *95, 109*
ansar 100-1, *103-4*
appliqué 99-102, 104-5, 108-9, 112, *12, 59, 99, 102, 104, 106, 108*
Arab: army 13; conquerors 20, 25, 93; empire 20; invasion 11, 22, 35, 93; writers 22, 23
Arguim 24
Armenian 111, 128
asherah nahuak 66
Asyut 34
Aswan 64
Atlas mountains 27, *116*; High Atlas 16, 35, 77, 116, 117, *30, 36, 86, 91, 117*; Middle Atlas *47*
Awash, river 27
Awdagawast (modern Tedgadawast) 13
Ayt Atta 115
Ayt Brahim *91*
Ayt Haddidu 28, 77
Ayt Morrhad *86*
Ayt Ouaouzguit *45, 47, 90*
Ayt Oumalou 117, *117*
Ayt Yazza *30, 36*
Azemmour 56
Azrou 139

Bab Zuwayla 105, 109
bakhnuq 34, 65, 115, *48*
al-Bakri 23, 31, 32
Bandiagara 23, 134
baniqa 55
Baqqara 100, 102, 104, *88, 102*
baraka 27, 28, 115, *79*
bariti 129
barmaqli 57
Bedouin 33, 36, 77, *12, 33, 84*
Beja 101, 102, *102*
belt 31, 41, 57, 66, 68, 73, 76, 77, 90, 91, 115, 116, 128, *40, 47, 67, 89*; see also hizam
Beni-Amer 101
Beni Mguild 47
Beni Ourain *85*
Berber: people 12, 13, 16, 35, 36, 65, 77; motifs 24, 25; textiles 24, 34
Bisharin 35, 101
Bizerte 69
Blackman, Winifred 28, 39, 64
blanket 24, 122, *23, 55*; see also kaasa, kerka
bobbin 136
bride 49, 53, 57, 61-81, *61, 63, 66, 68, 69, 72, 73, 75, 79, 81*; bath 72; family of 64, 66, 68, 70
bridegroom ('aris) 59, 61-81; family of 64, 65, 66, 71
button 53, 68, 113
Bynon, James 28, 44, *30, 36*

caftan 65, 76, *11, 69*
Cairo 21, 39, 72, 84, 92, 96, 105, 113, 134, *15, 105, 106, 108*
cape 128, 129, *120, 130*; see also lamd
Cape Bon 31, *59*
Cape Verde Islands 25, 40, *25*
carding 28, *30*
Carthage 12, 13; Carthaginian 12, 22, 56
Chad 134
Chebla 37
Chenini 112, 115, *114*
Chennells, Ellen 22, *21*

children, youths 61, 76, 102, 117, *19, 73, 103, 134*
Chinese, raw silk 31, 125
Christian 16, 56, 120, 121, 125; Christianity 13, 119; church 125
Churchill, Winston 101, 104
circumcision 56, 61, 69, 76, 80, 130
cloak 43, 70, 76, 77, 80, 90, 91, 112, *89, 90, 91*; see also akhnif, aljaravias, handira, shuqqa
clothing 18, 19, 53, 63, 64, 65, 66, 72, 109; animal skins 129, *130*; gifts of 64, 65, 66, 71; new status 77
coins 53, 113-14, *110*; five piastre 112; imitation 112, *110*; Maria Theresa dollar 128
colonial: influence 17; period 139
colour symbolism 65, 72, 75, 77, 81, 107, 112, 121, 129, 130, *47, 63, 66, 79, 86, 130*; black 130, *130*; red 66, 72, 73, 77, 130, *47, 61, 68, 79, 130*; white 64, 66, 81, 121, 129, *81, 130*; yellow 130, *47, 130*
comb 28, *41*
commerce 13, 52, 133, 134, 139; imports 12, 18, 97, 112; exports 17
Coptic 13, 19, 134, *134*
cotton 21, 27, 29-31, 100, 115, 121, 129; bolls 29, 31; bowing, duggar (dagan) 29; ginning, medamager (madamacha) 29, 30; plant 29; tet 29
Crowfoot, Grace 28, 29, 31, 35
cushion cover 106, *18, 108*
Cyrenaica 12

Damascus 133
darawish 100-1, 103-4, *100*
Darfur 100, *88*
death 59, 121, 129, 130, *130*
dejazmach 129, *130*
derfudit 92, *15*
Djebala 115
Dorze 120, 121, 129, 130, 136, 137, *130*
dress 114, 122, 124, *12, 79, 83, 92, 109, 110*; see also asherah nahuak, girgar, kamis, wedding
dunguse 129, *130*
dyeing 32-3, *27*; resist-dyeing 65, 99, 112, 114-15, 125, *48, 63, 114, 115*; tie-and-dye 115, *43*
dyes 27, 32-3; analine 32, 33, 117, 130, 139; indigo 32; natural 32, 33

education 83-4, 88, *88*
Egypt 11, 12, 13, 17-21, 23, 31, 38, 41, 52, 63, 64, 72, 76, 90-1, 93, 97, 105, 107, 112, 136, *20, 21, 59, 81, 95*; Upper 28, 32, 35, 39, 114, 136, *35*; Western Desert 28, 32, 36, 39, 77, 99, 112, 116, 117, 134, *92, 93, 110*
El-Jem 49, 116
embroidery 18, 20, 30, 31, 48-9, 52-3, 55-6, 65, 68, 70, 80, 91-2, 99, 109, 111-15, 125, 137, *18-19, 43, 47, 63, 71, 75, 79, 90, 109, 111, 124-6*
employment 88-9
engagement 72; gifts 70; see also milak, waddah
English 96, 125
Ethiopia 29, 38, 41, 99, 109, 119-25, 128-30, 136-7, 139, *31, 39, 119, 126, 130, 137*
Europe 17, 25; European 12, 17, 21, 22, 24, 80, 81, 92, 96, *21, 81, 88*
evil eye ('ayn) 27, 43, 44, 47, 53, 57, 76, 80, 104, 117, 121, 129, *104*

Falasha 121, 128
faltita 16
farmala 93
farrash 105
fatiha ceremony 65
Fatimids 13, 16, 20, 105, *20*
Fedija 49, 64
female: activities 28, 55, 63; costumes 57, 61, 63, 76, 83; honour 73, 76; weaving 34, 136, 139, *35*
fertility 24, 49, 53, 56, 61, 69, 70, 72-7, *49, 66, 79*
Fes 20, 31, 32, 34, 39, 40, 41, 56, 57, 69, 111, *11, 18, 40, 41, 67, 72*
fish 44, 52, 53, 57, *43, 49, 75*
flag, banner 104, 105, *104*
French 17, 96, 139, *40*

Gabes 31, 32, 48, 65, 115, *48*
gallabiya 89, 96, 97, 134, *93*
Gamu Gofa Highlands 120, 129, *130*
gandura 47, *87*
Garamantes 13
Gaza 40
Ghana 123, 137, 139
Gharyan 115, *115*

girgar 64
goblan 134
Gondar 31, 120, 121, 125, 128, *126, 128*
gonfa 129
Granada 16; fall of 56
guild 120, 128
Guinea Bissau 25, 40
Gulf War 107

hadana ceremony 77
Hadendoa 101
Hafsids 16
hair 77, 116, *43*
halakas 85
Hammamet 111, *109*
handira 85, *86*
hantoz 80
Harraniya 134, *134*
hat 117, *117*
Hausa 52, 104, *15*
headwear 77, 84, 115, *15*; cap 55, 77, 96, see also baniqa, taqiya; head-cloth (almarfad) 80; head-dress 77, 116; head-shawl 48, *43*
Heathcote, David 52
henna 72, 75, *61, 79*
higab 84; muhaggaba 85
Hispano-Moresque 25, 40, 57, 67
hizam 57, *47, 67*; see also belt
hizama ceremony 75

Ibn Hawkal 31
Ibn Khaldun 20, 23
Ifriqiya 13, 16, 21
Imilchil Plateau 77
India 13, 76
Islam: beliefs 44, 69; conversion 11, 13; Islamic 19, 61; spread of 11, 13, 43

jacket 57, 96, *45, 71, 86*; see also kumbayz
jallaba 96
jarbiya 68
Jews 57, 68, 69, 111, 121, *70, 90*; Jewish 31-2, 41, 69, 80, 92, 93, 96, 128, *71*
jihad 99, 100, 101
jilwa 57, 72, 69
jird 76
jirtiq 73, 75, *76*
Johnston, Charles 29-30; jubbat al-'ayn fil-'ayn 57; jubba matruza 11, 109
jubba 76, 99-105, 112, *102-4*; jubbat al-'ayn fil-'ayn 57; jubba matruza 11, 109

kaasa 23, 24
Kafr el-Elow 70, 89
Kairouan 59
kamis 122, 124, 126, 127
Kano 52
katfiya 34, 112, 115, *114*
katif 96
kente 123, 137
Kenuz 70, 77, 80
Kerdassa 40, 92, 134, *15*
kerka 24, *22*
Khalifa 99, 100, 101, 103, 105, *102*
khamsa 44
Khartoum 73, 99, 100
khila' 19
khiyamiya 105-9, *105, 107*; see also siwan and suradiq
kilim trabelsi 7
kiswat al-kabira 96, *71*
knitting 99, 116, 117, *117*
Konson 121, 129, 130, 137, *130*
Kordofan 99, 100
Ksour el-Saf 49
Kuba 104
kumbayz 96
kutta see shamma

lailat al-dukhla 69, 70, 76
lailat al-hinna' 76, *79*
lamba 123
lambens 24
lamd 128, 129, *120, 130*
Lane, Edward 21, 72, 90, 93, 116
Libya 17, 48, 52, 65, 68, 93, 115, 116, 134, *15, 63, 95, 115, 134*; Libyans 136, *7*
life-style 84, 91, 100; change 35, 139
limut see shamma
linen 18, 31, *20*
lion 59

loom 33–41; Berber 36–8, 139; double-heddle 40, 23, 29; draw 39–40, 40, 67; ground 35–6, 139, 36–7; Jacquard 40; metal 139, 33, 139; pit 38–9, 38; single-heddle 34–6, 115, 139, 37; tablet 41, 41; treadle 34, 38–41, 134, 136, 35, 39, 95, 134; tripod 39; vertical 34, 36, 7, 90
Luxor 39

machine technology 119, 136; factory-printed 107, 108; milled cloth 137
Madagascar 123
Maghrib, definition of 11, 16, 17, 25
Mahdi 16, 99–101, 101; Mahdism 100; Mahdist 100–104, 112, 102, 103; Mahdiya 100, 101, 104
Mahdia 13
male activities 28; costumes 57, 61, 63, 76, 83; embroidery 48, 52, 90, 126; honour 64; knitting 117; weaving 34, 38, 41, 136, 35, 95
Manchester 125
Mandinka 25
Manjaka 40
al-Maqrizi 105
Marinid 16, 21
markets 134, 136, 139, 134; see also suq
Marrakesh 16, 33, 27
marriage 24, 49, 55, 61–81, 22, 47, 79; ceremony 49, 69–72; costume 52, 53, 57, 59, 65, 68, 72, 49, 79; dress 64, 65, 68, 70, 80, 81, 112, 81; dowry 64, 65; forty days 80; knots 73, 76; payment 64, 65, 70, 72; seventh day 27, 65, 73, 75, 76, 80; third day 4, 66, 75
mashita 68, 69
Masqal 130
materials: glass 129; gold thread 52, 57, 65, 80, 92, 96, 49, 63; lurex 32, 35, 126; metal braid 65, 92, 111, 129, 71; prohibition of 19, 20; protection 27; silk thread 55, 73, 75, 92, 96, 20; silver thread 65, 92; velvet 80, 128, 55, 70, 71, 129, 130
Mecca 11, 21
Meknes 37
Mende 39
Middle East 11, 35, 52, 93, 97
milak 66
milaya 95
modesty: code 64, 89; concerns about 63, 84, 92, 97, 92; garments 64, 84, 88, 89, 91, 96, 99, 136, 92, 95, 134
Moknine 57
Monastir 49
Moorish 25, 93, 25
Morocco 13, 16, 17, 24, 33, 41, 57, 59, 66, 69, 76, 80, 93, 96, 99, 105, 109, 117, 128, 11, 16, 45, 47, 67, 68, 86, 89
mu'allim 57
mu'allima 55
muraqqa'a 100, 101, 103, 104, 100, 102
Muslim 11, 39
Mzab 47, 68, 69, 87

Nabeul 57
naggafa 69
Naqada 31, 136, 35, 95, 133, 134
Niger 22; river 22, 23
Nigeria 11, 29, 32, 99, 104, 115, 125, 136, 139, 15
Nile, river 11, 27; Delta 31, 33, 34, 40, 64, 80, 33; Valley 27, 29, 34, 38, 40, 104, 112, 114
Nubia 48–9, 52, 70, 77, 59; Nubians 64

oasis 52; Bahriya 92, 112–14, 116–17, 136, 79, 110, 113, 116, 134; Dakhla 112, 79; Farafra 28, 112, 117; Ghadames 49, 52, 68, 70, 77, 116, 15, 63, 79; Kharga 112, 113–14; Siwa 5, 12, 31, 53, 68, 72, 80, 92, 112, 113, 134, 15, 47, 63, 66, 75
Omdurman 28, 35, 73, 76, 77, 101, 102, 105; battle of 100, 105
Oran 24
Ottoman 16, 17, 21, 109
Ouaouzguit 90
Oudref 33
Oued Zem 139

Palestine 35, 40, 112
Parkyns, Mansfield 122, 123, 124, 125
passementerie 68, 111, 109
patchwork 105; patches 99–101, 103–5
patterns 23, 40–1, 43–59, 92, 108, 115, 22, 23, 45; animals 19, 48, 49, 52, 105, 7, 19, 20, 43, 49, 139; eight-pointed star 25, 56, 57, 43, 49; hand 44, 53, 56, 57, 43, 47, 55, 59; humans 18, 56, 105, 125, 49, 139; names 24, 47, 48, 55, 87
Phoenicians 12, 13, 56
Picton and Mack 28, 29, 35, 37, 38, 101, 104, 33

pillow 117
plaiting 99, 116, 117, 116; tress 116
plastic 136
plastron 52, 53, 68, 96, 55, 71
pocket 101, 103, 104, 104
Portugal 16, 40; Portuguese 16, 24, 25, 40, 56, 134, 25
Prophet Muhammad 19, 100, 101, 107
puberty 64, 83

qaftan 93; see also caftan
qamajja 57
qarmasis 76
quilting 104, 105
Qur'an 19, 53, 103, 104, 107, 104
qurbab 77

Rabat 55, 71
Raf-Raf 52, 4, 49, 75
rag-work 39, 136
Ramses Wissa Wassef 134, 134
Rashaida 102, 112, 12, 122
raw materials 89, 121; camel hair 27, 28; dwarf palm 31; esparto grass 31; flax 31, 19; goat hair 27, 28, 21, 23; kapok 105; palm leaf 115; rush 31
rayon 31, 34, 136, 35, 38, 119, 126, 134
Red Sea 13; Arabs 101, 102; ports 76, 120; Province 101
Redeyef 7
rida' al-halib 65
robe 18, 19, 90, 128, 136; see also gallabiya, jallaba
Roman 13, 19
Rufa'a 38
Rugh, Andrea 96, 112
rural 11, 23, 43, 44–53, 56, 65, 69, 70, 83, 89–90

saddlebag 117
Sa'dians 17, 25
Safi 24, 25
safsari 89
sash see belt
Saudi Arabia 107, 12
Second World War 17, 31
sequins 57, 65, 70, 77, 80, 92, 117, 75, 79, 129
seven 53, 72, 75, 76, 80, 75
Sfax 65, 72
shamma 122–5, 129, 136, 139, 39, 119, 120, 121, 123, 126; buluko 122; kutta 122; limut 122, 124; natala 122, 124, 137; tibeb 122, 123, 136, 39, 119, 120, 121
Shawa province 29, 119
Shawiya 37
shawl 24, 48, 49, 65, 76, 80, 91, 99, 112, 122, 15, 47, 48, 63, 85, 86, 137; see also bakhnuq, buluko, derfudit, handira, kutta, milaya, natala, qarmasis, ta'jira
shed stick 36, 37, 39
shintiyan 21, 96, 93
shoulder-cloth 48, 112, 115; see also ta'jira
shroud 57, 59, 122, 4, 119
shuqqa 77
shuttle, boat 136, 38; flying shuttle 40
Sidama 137, 130
Sidamo province 120
sidar 93
Sierra Leone 39
Sijilmasa 21, 23
Sinai 112
siwan 105, 106
skirt 96, 12, 16, 71; see also faltita
smatt see saddlebag
smock 129, 130, 137
social: class 19, 21, 85, 92, 96, 120, 122, 11; control 66; discrimination 63, 121, 129; dress as communication 64, 122; insignia 103; mobility 85, 88; rank 101, 103, 120, 122, 128; status 20, 77, 80, 89, 93, 96, 104, 120, 122, 123, 95
Songhay 17
Sousse 65
Spain 12, 13, 16, 25, 40, 56, 25; Spanish 17, 20, 25, 96, 111, 16, 70
spindle, drop-spindle 28
spinning 28, 29, 30, 31, 30, 31
starch 115
Sudan 11, 28, 29, 35, 38, 61, 64, 69, 70, 73, 76, 77, 80, 84, 88, 89, 99, 100, 102, 112, 134, 12, 38, 95, 134
Suez Canal 17
suf 100; see also wool
Sufi 99, 100, 100, 102
sulphur 139
suq 90; suq al-khiyamia 105, 107

suradiq 105; see also tent
Sus 25
synthetic fibres 31, 125
Syria 13, 19, 19, 133

ta'am 70
table cloth 137
tahzim ceremony 76
ta'jira 34, 115
takhlila 89
tal 57, 79
Tana, Lake 128
Tangier 13, 24, 70
tanshifa 55, 43
taqiya 96
tarha 49, 88
tariqa 100
Tataouine 65
tattoo 48; mwashma 4, 41, 75
Tawzar 32
Tegré 119, 120, 122, 124, 120, 121, 126
telli 114
tent 37, 99, 105, 106, 30, 37, 99, 106; flij 37; tent cloth 35, 65, 139, 22, 36, 59; tent maker see khiyamiya; see also siwan, suradiq
Testour 56, 95
Tetouan 57, 70
tha'ban 70, 76, 117
thawb 64, 70, 76, 84, 88, 88
al-Tijani 21, 32
tiraz 20, 105; dar al-tiraz 20; tiraz al-'amm 20
Tlemcen 41, 69
tourism 106, 107, 134, 136
towel 111, 18
trade 12, 13, 22, 25, 40, 128, 134, 23; animal hides 12; camel transport 13; gold 12, 13, 16, 25; goods 76; ivory 13; posts 12, 24; routes 18, 52, 15; trans-Saharan 12, 13, 17, 22, 23, 24, 134, 15
Tripoli 16, 17, 71, 75
Tripolitania 12, 13, 22, 47, 7
trousers 75, 76, 80, 93, 96, 117, 124, 125, 129, 130, 137, 75, 92, 93, 125, 130; see also bariti, dunguse, gonfa, shintiyan, tha'ban
trousseau 64, 65, 70, 72
tunic 18, 52, 57, 59, 65, 90, 93, 100, 124, 125, 4, 19, 49, 75, 79, 87, 100, 102; see also gandura, jubba, qamajja
Tunisia 13, 17, 27, 31, 33, 44, 45, 47, 48, 65, 66, 68, 70, 72, 89, 93, 99, 109, 112, 134, 4, 7, 43, 63, 79, 95
Turkish 17, 21, 53, 56, 57, 92, 93, 96, 111, 43, 93
Tutankhamun 18, 107, 19

Umayyad 13, 16, 19, 20
uniform 88, 100, 101, 102
'uqus 116, 117
urban 11, 21, 41, 43, 53, 55, 68, 69, 80, 83–5, 88, 92–3, 96–7, 137, 95
Uthman dan Fodio 99
Uthman Diqna 101, 102

veil 49, 52, 56, 57, 64, 65, 77, 80, 88, 112, 4, 61, 68, 81, 95; see also rida' al-halib, 'ajar, tarha
versalia 134
vestment 125
Volubolis 37

waddah 70; see also engagement
waistcoat 93, 49; see also farmala, sidar
wall-hanging 125, 4
warp 37, 38, 41, 41; laying of 37, 40
weaver 37, 136, 39; protection of 44; rituals 45; rural 44–5
weaving 28; slit-tapestry 47, 86; tablet 31, 92, 125, 128, 126, 128; tapestry 18, 19, 115, 117, 134, 136, 19, 20, 87, 97, 134
wedding see marriage
West Africa 11, 24, 39, 40, 49, 52, 114, 134, 139
wheat 115, 115
Wolof 25
wool 21, 23, 27–9, 100, 115, 21, 23, 30; see also suf

yawm al-dukhla 70, 76
Yemen 128
Yoruba 115, 125; patterns 32

Zaire 104
zaltita 96
Zayan 117
Zemmour 33, 55
Zirids 13
ziyy islami 84